The Invisible Investor

How to Build Freedom and Fortune through Real Estate You Never Own

By Jay R. Pocius

First edition.

EBook: 978-1-970686-14-2

Paperback: 978-1-970686-12-8

Overview

The Invisible Investor redefines what it means to be a real estate investor in a world where control, influence, and digital leverage are often more powerful than title or deed.

This book is about profiting from real estate without owning property by learning to control opportunity, relationships, and systems.

It's a roadmap for agents, entrepreneurs, and investors who want to build generational wealth through a proven, solid strategy.

Dedication

To those who build quietly.

To the dreamers who don't need the spotlight, to the creators who see opportunity in chaos, and the investors who design freedom without fanfare.

This book is for every person who believes that wealth isn't about what you own; it's about what you create, control, and contribute.

May your systems outlast your effort, your partnerships outgrow your plans, and your freedom arrive sooner than you expected.

— Jay R. Pocius

Contents

A Note from the Author

When I first began my journey in real estate, I believed what most of us were taught to believe, that success meant ownership. Ownership was the finish line. It was the proof that all the late nights, open houses, and closings had paid off. If you owned property, multiple properties, you'd "made it."

For years, that was the goal. I bought condos, managed tenants, oversaw renovations, and experienced everything that comes with ownership: the excitement, the leverage, and eventually, the weight. I loved the work, but over time, something shifted. I started to notice that the more I owned, the less free I became.

Every new property added another layer of responsibility: more repairs, more management, more stress. What once represented independence began to feel like infrastructure, solid, yes, but also heavy.

And I began to ask myself a question that would eventually change my entire outlook on wealth: If every asset I own requires more of my time, energy, and capital just to keep alive, is it truly an asset? Or is it simply a more sophisticated form of dependency? That question became the seed of what you now hold in your hands.

The Moment the Pattern Became Clear

Before acquiring my brokerage, I worked in land acquisition and development for one of the largest homebuilders in the country. I saw, up close, how billions of dollars in real estate were created and controlled, and it was not always through ownership.

Developers would flip entitlement rights. Builders would pre-sell projects before breaking ground. Investors would fund deals they never physically touched. Meanwhile, digital platforms like Airbnb and WeWork were rewriting the entire playbook.

They were controlling real estate without owning it, and they were outpacing legacy owners who had been collecting deeds for decades. That realization hit me hard: the biggest returns in real estate were no longer tied to property, but to position. The ones who controlled the deal flow, the data, and the distribution: they were the real power players.

In every corner of the industry, a quiet revolution was underway. A new type of investor was emerging. The kind who built systems, not storage; leverage, not liability. They were earning profit and equity through access, creativity, and control rather than capital. They were invisible to most, but they were everywhere.

Why I Wrote This Book

I wrote The Invisible Investor because I believe that we are standing on the edge of one of the biggest shifts in the history of real estate, a shift from possession to participation. The old investor model said, “Own everything.” The new model says, “Control what matters.”

And control today doesn’t require capital: it involves knowledge, relationships, and design. Many people still believe that the only way to build wealth in real estate is to buy property. But look closer and you will see that wealth is created every day by people who don’t own anything in the traditional sense.

- The property manager who scales her portfolio through master leases instead of mortgages.
- The agent who earns recurring revenue through marketing rights, not commission checks.
- The lender who structures equity participation instead of origination fees.
- The digital creator whose local housing website generates passive leads for investors.

These people aren’t anomalies: they’re the future. And I wanted to write the guide that shows exactly how and why this works.

This book is my blueprint for that evolution: a map for building real estate wealth through systems of control, not stacks of debt.

The New Definition of Real Estate Investor

You don't need millions in capital to be an investor anymore. You need clarity, creativity, and collaboration. You need to understand that "equity" now takes many forms: digital, relational, intellectual, and systemic.

Your brand can be an asset. Your database can be an asset. Your reputation, your process, your network: all can generate wealth just as property does, if not more. The Invisible Investor sees what others miss: that ownership is not the goal: leverage is. And leverage today does not come from deeds. It comes from design.

Who This Book Is For

- For the real estate agent tired of starting every month at zero.
- For the lender, designer, or contractor who knows their expertise deserves long-term upside.
- For the digital marketer or creator who wants to apply their skills to an asset class that never stops moving.
- For the investor who feels priced out but refuses to be left out.

This book gives you the frameworks, models, and mindset to start building your invisible portfolio: the one that grows through relationships, ideas & systems.

A Framework for Freedom

Inside, you will learn how four archetypes of the Invisible Investor create and scale wealth:

- The Connector, who monetizes relationships and information.
- The Controller, who manages and operates property owned by others.
- The Creator, who builds digital real estate, marketing funnels, platforms, and brand ecosystems that drive deal flow.
- The Collaborator, who trades skills for equity in high-value projects.

Each path has one thing in common: they all create ownership-like outcomes without the weight of ownership itself. You'll learn how to design systems that work for you, systems that continue generating income and influence even when you are not actively working.

A Philosophy for the Next Generation

You don't have to own the world to shape it. You don't have to control property to control your destiny. And you don't need to wait for capital to build leverage: you just need to recognize the value of what you already control.

In this new era, wealth isn't about accumulation: it's about architecture. It's not about what you can afford; it's about what you can design. That's what invisible investing really means: freedom through systems, equity through creativity, and legacy through design.

A Final Word

I have seen firsthand what happens when people stop chasing ownership and start building control. Their income stabilizes. Their stress declines. Their creativity explodes. They become the architects of their lives, not the caretakers of their assets.

If you remember nothing else from this book, remember this: Ownership used to mean security. Now, it often means limitation. Freedom isn't about how much you hold: it's about how much you can release and remain in control.

Welcome to the future of wealth. Welcome to the Invisible Investor.

— Jay R. Pocius

Introduction: The Death of the Deed

For generations, ownership sat at the center of the American wealth story. If you did not have deeds with your name on them, you were not building a future. That worked when homes were affordable, debt was manageable, and appreciation felt steady. Owning assets was logical.

That world has shifted. Prices climbed, wages flattened, and the time cost of managing physical assets rose. A digital economy emerged that rewards speed, creativity, influence, and access over possession. People now build real income with a laptop, a brand, and the right partners. They earn from systems rather than structures, from platforms rather than properties, and from relationships rather than mortgages.

The End of the Old Dream

For more than a century, the phrase “owning property” has been a universal measure of success. It was the heartbeat of the American Dream, a symbol of stability, freedom, and wealth. From the white picket fence to the downtown skyscraper, we were taught that ownership equals power.

The logic was simple. If you own it, you control it. But that equation no longer holds true. In today’s economy, the most powerful companies and wealthiest entrepreneurs don't own much at all. They control, influence, and orchestrate, but they rarely hold titles.

Uber doesn't own cars. Airbnb doesn't own the homes. WeWork didn't own the office towers that made it famous. Even Amazon, the world's largest retailer, owns only a fraction of the products it sells.

Control has replaced ownership as the defining currency of wealth. And that same shift has quietly entered the world of real estate.

The quiet part is that success no longer looks like a list of addresses. Many effective operators do not own anything they touch. They control access, relationships, and deal flow. They earn from influence, marketing systems, operational skill, and the ability to direct opportunity. In a control-based world, wealth is not what you hold. It is what you can activate.

The Rise of the Control Economy

The digital revolution didn't just disrupt industries; it rewired the very concept of asset. An asset used to mean something tangible: a house, a building, a factory. Today, assets are systems: algorithms, audiences, brand equity, data pipelines.

They generate predictable income, but they don't sit on land. The Control Economy was born when technology made it possible to access and monetize resources without owning them. Streaming replaced CDs. Subscriptions replaced purchases.

Platforms replaced storefronts. Real estate, once considered immune to this shift, is now at the forefront of it. Airbnb built a global hospitality network without a single hotel. Zillow became a data empire without selling houses. Compass created one of the largest agent networks in the country without owning a single brokerage building. Ownership has become optional, and often, it's a liability.

The real value now lies in control points: data, relationships, contracts, and brand authority. The invisible investor understands this. They don't chase property lines, but build systems that profit from the flow of value across them.

The Myth of the Deed

A deed is just a piece of paper, proof that you legally own something. But that ownership comes with weight: debt, taxes, liability, and volatility. Ask any landlord navigating a shifting market or dealing with rising interest rates, maintenance, and turnover.

The asset may be tangible, but so are the headaches. Meanwhile, a short-term rental operator who controls twenty units through master leases may earn more than the landlord who owns them, and with far less risk.

Similarly, a marketing firm that licenses its real estate lead systems to multiple brokerages may create a passive cash flow equivalent to owning several rental properties, but without mortgages or maintenance.

How Technology Changed Asset Control

To understand the power of invisible investing, you have to understand how technology quietly democratized access. Before, real estate investing was gated by capital and credit. Now, it's gated by knowledge. The investor who understands contracts, marketing systems, and operational control has more leverage than the one who brings cash alone.

Digitizing attention: Social platforms, SEO, and email marketing gave individuals control over audiences that once cost millions to reach.

Automating value: CRMs, AI, and online marketplaces allowed small operators to manage at scale with minimal staff.

Democratizing partnerships: Smart contracts, fractional ownership, and revenue-sharing models made collaboration frictionless.

Together, these forces made it possible to build wealth without ever signing a closing document. The gatekeepers lost their monopoly on opportunity. And in their place, a new class of investors emerged: agile, creative, and unseen.

The Operator of Opportunity

- A digital marketer builds a city-specific website that ranks for local home searches, selling those leads to agents and lenders for recurring revenue.
- A property operator signs long-term leases on apartments, rebrands them as furnished units, and

captures the margin between rent and sublet income.

- A contractor renovates properties in exchange for a share of profits instead of flat fees: accumulating equity without investment.
- A consultant advises a real estate group in exchange for revenue participation, building a portfolio of passive stakes across projects.
- None of these people owns the underlying properties. But all of them earn from them. They are operators of opportunity.

Why Ownership is Slowing You Down

Ownership has become the new debt trap. In a world that moves faster than ever, owning something fixed can limit your flexibility. Landlords are tied to local economies, regulations, and tax changes.

Homeowners can't pivot when opportunities shift. Meanwhile, the control-based investor can reallocate instantly: pivoting from management to marketing to licensing, across markets and industries. They can,

- Scale without banks.
- Profit without property.
- Build wealth through collaboration instead of accumulation.

This doesn't mean ownership is obsolete: it means it's no longer required. It's one option in a much larger portfolio of possibilities.

That is why this book exists. Most people still chase the old blueprint and wonder why the finish line moves. The real opportunity now lives outside the walls of ownership. The most valuable assets in modern real estate are not buildings. They are systems, relationships, data, audiences, credibility, and control.

This is a practical guide to that world. It invites you to redefine your identity as an investor, not by counting deeds but by mastering leverage. You will learn how creators, negotiators, operators, and strategists quietly profit behind the scenes. The wealth may not show on a property report, yet it shows in the bank.

The Four Archetypes of the Invisible Investor

1. **The Connector**: The master networker who earns by creating value through relationships, referrals, and introductions.
2. **The Controller**: The operational strategist who earns from management contracts, master leases, and revenue-sharing systems.
3. **The Creator**: The digital architect who builds online platforms, funnels, and audiences that monetize real estate through attention and data.
4. **The Collaborator**: The professional who trades specialized expertise for equity or profit participation instead of a one-time paycheck.

Each path offers a different route to the same destination: recurring income without ownership.

The Invisible Revolution

We are moving from a world of possession to a world of participation. The barriers to entry are lower than ever, but so is the margin for mediocrity.

Winners will be data literate, digitally fluent, and partnership-oriented. They'll build leverage through collaboration and operate in ecosystems rather than empires.

The Invisible Investor's Creed

- Ownership is optional. Control is what counts.
- Equity isn't always financial. It can be intellectual, digital, or relational.
- Freedom comes from structure. Systems and contracts create flexibility, not chaos.
- Leverage is infinite when trust is scalable. Empower others, and your influence compounds.

Your Role in the Next Chapter

- Build wealth through systems you control but don't own.
- Turn digital assets and relationships into recurring revenue.
- Create invisible equity through collaboration and influence.
- Design exit strategies based on intellectual property instead of property titles.

The Death of the Deed

In the modern economy, leverage is invisible; found in data, contracts, communities, and code. The most successful investors of the next decade will master access, automation, and alignment.

If the old world taught us that ownership is everything, the new world offers something better. Ownership is optional. Control creates mobility. Influence creates scale. Systems create freedom.

With that understanding, we can look back at the mythology of ownership and why it fails the modern builder. That reflection begins in Chapter One.

The End of Ownership

The idea of ownership still holds power in our imagination. Many of us were raised to believe that buying property is a rite of passage into legitimacy. Ownership signals stability and progress, yet it also carries invisible burdens that only appear after the ink dries.

The environment that once made ownership straightforward has changed. Volatility increased. Insurance and taxes rose faster than income. Cycles move harder and with less warning. The modern economy rewards flexibility more than permanence, which pushes many investors to seek control without weight.

The Myth of the American Dream

For most of the 20th century, wealth in America followed a single, simple formula: Work → Save → Buy → Own. Owning property wasn't just a financial goal; it was a moral one.

But that dream was designed for an economy that no longer exists. Today's market is defined by speed, volatility, and access, and the idea that freedom depends on owning physical property has become a limiting belief.

In the mid-century economy, careers were linear, interest rates were stable for long stretches, and mobility was lower. The social contract rewarded staying put.

In today's economy, opportunity shifts faster than capital can. That makes flexibility a competitive advantage, not a consolation prize.

The Hidden Cost of Ownership

Every deed carries invisible costs. Ownership locks up capital, limits flexibility, and transfers responsibility for risk. Control-based investors use a better equation: Control → Leverage → Scale → Freedom.

Instead of buying an asset, they buy a position in the system that uses the asset: profiting from access rather than accumulation. A master lease operator can often match a landlord's cash flow with a fraction of capital and risk, and exit quickly if conditions change.

Think of two investors. One ties up $200,000 in a down payment to net $12,000 per month. The other deploys $10,000 in furnishings and deposits to control the same income through a master lease. Both earn cash flow. Only one remains liquid enough to pivot when conditions change.

There is also emotional load that never appears in a pro forma. Investors watch rates and wonder if they mistimed entry. They worry about surprise repairs and vacancies. They manage tenants, contractors, and a wave of local rules that keep growing. The math may be tight on paper while the mind pays a premium every week.

Freedom Flow Formula

Value Created

How much impact you generate

×

Leverage Retained

How much control you keep

=

Weight Carried

True much cost or risk you hold

Freedom

True wealth: control without constraint

©JAY R. POCIUS | THE INVISIBLE INVESTOR

Beyond emotion, capital tied to title often underperforms compared to capital tied to control. A six-figure down payment on one rental might produce modest cash flow after debt, taxes, insurance, and repairs. The same capital, pointed at a lead funnel, a master lease, or a service for equity agreement, can earn more with less exposure. The asset is not always the building. Often it is the ecosystem around the building.

Going From Ownership to Access

- You don't buy CDs: you stream.
- You don't buy taxis: you summon them.

- You don't buy servers: you rent cloud capacity.

Real estate mirrors this shift. Platforms control access to inventory, data, and demand: a position often worth more than ownership.

Access reduces time to impact. The less you need to acquire before you can operate, the faster you can test, learn, and scale what works.

Control Will Always Outperform Ownership

Ownership delivers security. Control delivers velocity. And in modern markets, velocity compounds faster than stability.

Asset-light models in hospitality, brokerage networks, digital platforms, and service partnerships prove the point.

A useful sanity check: if better execution can change the outcome faster than market appreciation can, you are in a control business. If results depend mostly on time, you are in an ownership business.

The Psychology of Letting Go

The hardest part is emotional. Ownership feels safe and tangible. But adaptability is the new safety. Letting go of ownership isn't giving up: it's moving up.

Loss aversion and status signaling make titles feel more valuable than they are. Reframe the goal from "own more stuff" to "own more outcomes." What you can change on demand is worth more than what you can only hold.

Part of the grip on ownership is cultural. People learned that title equals success, so the reflex is to keep chasing it. That reflex no longer matches the landscape. The cost of entry is higher, the risk is greater, and the margin is thinner, while the opportunities outside of ownership are more abundant than at any time in recent memory. Letting go is not giving up. It is moving into alignment with how value really moves.

The Asset Light Advantage

- **Airbnb and the Experience Economy**: curation and brand trust create value faster than construction.
- **eXp Realty and Digital Brokerage**: cloud-based operations scale without physical offices.
- **Sonder and Corporate Housing**: operational control outperforms owned asset portfolios in agility.
- **Blackstone and Institutional Scale**: fees and carry are mechanisms of control over capital, not just deeds.

The pattern across these examples is consistent. Separate the real estate from the revenue engine, then scale the engine. Systems multiply. Buildings slow down.

The Control Equation

Control + Systems = Compounding Leverage.

Traditional investors scale as fast as their money allows. Invisible investors scale as fast as their systems allow.

Three questions expose your control points,

- What inputs can I set?
- What processes can I standardize?
- What outputs can I measure weekly?

If you can set, standardize, and measure it, you can scale it.

Control based models scale by creativity and system strength rather than by credit and down payment. Once you see this distinction, the field opens. You stop asking what you can buy and start asking what you can influence, operate, or control. That single shift is what unlocks compounding outcomes.

The Ownership Trap

Ownership still has value when strategic. But the title is no longer the ultimate proof of wealth; flow is. Who controls lead flow, data flow, and revenue flow? That's where scalable wealth resides.

Flow beats stock. A list of qualified buyers, a calendar full of bookings, or a pipeline of warm introductions can be worth more than a deed when velocity matters.

The Shift Already Happening

The invisible investor builds systems around what others buy: connecting people, properties, and profits. They own the map, not the terrain.

- Lenders monetizing data instead of loans.
- Agents building personal brands that out-earn brokerages.
- Property managers turning service contracts into recurring income portfolios.
- Marketers licensing ad systems instead of selling one-time services.

Field Exercise: Map Your Control Points

List the five places in your current work where you can influence outcomes without owning the asset.

For each, write one action that increases control next week: a clearer contract, a standard operating procedure, a pricing rule, or a reporting dashboard.

Looking Ahead

Picture the industry as a network of visible and hidden entry points. Title is only one of them. The Invisible Investor steps into the space between ownership and outcome.

Next, we'll explore the four archetypes: Connector, Controller, Creator, and Collaborator, and help you identify the path that fits your strengths.

As you read, keep a running tally of where you already exercise control. That is your fastest path to invisible equity.

The Four Paths of the Invisible Investor

Introduction: Four Roads to Freedom

Every investor wants the same three things: freedom, income, and impact. But how they get there depends on what they can control.

Modern real estate is an ecosystem with many roles, and only a few require ownership. The four archetypes in this chapter, the Connector, the Controller, the Creator, and the Collaborator, map the most leverage-rich routes used by profitable operators today. They are not a theory. They are working models that turn position into cash flow.

Traditional investing ties control to ownership. You buy a property; you believe you control the outcome. Invisible investing ties control to position. You do not need the deed. You need influence over the value that moves through the system.

Invisible investors build wealth by mastering leverage points inside the real estate ecosystem. There are many ways to do it, yet most winning plays trace back to four core archetypes.

- **The Connector**: the network architect who turns relationships and information into revenue.
- **The Controller**: the operator who runs and improves assets that other people own.

- **The Creator**: the digital strategist who builds and monetizes online assets that steer demand and deal flow.
- **The Collaborator**: the expert who trades skill and judgment for equity rather than a one-time fee.

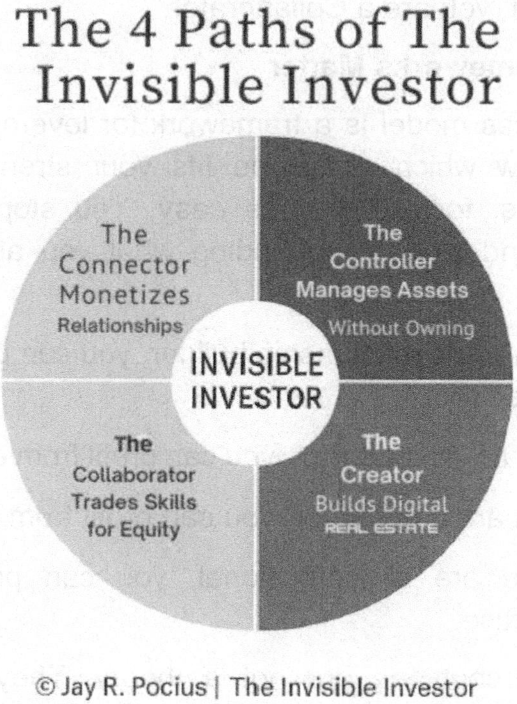

Each archetype concentrates a different kind of power. The Connector focuses relationships. The Controller focuses operations. The Creator focuses attention. The Collaborator focuses expertise. Seen together, they form a complete picture of how value moves through the industry without a deed.

Each path leads to invisible wealth. Each one lets you profit from value without owning the vessel.

A quick way to choose your starting lane: If people call you first, you are a Connector. If people call you when things break, you are a Controller. If people find you online, you are a Creator. If people hire you for judgment, you are a Collaborator.

Why Frameworks Matter

A business model is a framework for leverage. Once you know which archetype fits your strengths and resources, focus becomes easy. You stop chasing trends and start compounding what you already do well.

- If you are a relationship builder, you can profit from connectivity.
- If you are an operator, you can profit from efficiency.
- If you are a marketer, you can profit from attention.
- If you are a professional, you can profit from expertise.

These archetypes are not a theory. They are the engines behind much of the modern real estate economy. Chances are you already lean toward one of them, even if you have not named it yet.

Let us break them down, one by one.

Understanding these paths is also a psychological shift. Most readers recognize themselves in one lane or in parts of several. That recognition is leverage. You stop forcing a single identity onto a rigid model and start matching your natural strengths to the role that multiplies them.

The Connector: Turning Relationships into Revenue

The Connector is the orchestrator. The work is not about buildings. It is about people, timing, and trust. Wealth comes from knowing who to call, when to call, and how to create a match that benefits both sides.

This role used to live only with agents and brokers. Today, it lives inside digital communities, referral networks, private groups, and data ecosystems that never sleep. The Connector thrives on access and the credibility that earns access again.

For years, Connectors were influential but underpaid. Digital platforms changed that. Referrals can be tracked, conversions measured, and agreements documented. The person who brings the right people together now captures real, recurring value.

Picture this. A buyer asks for a lender with creative options. A seller needs a staging team on short notice. A developer wants a partner who can fill a building with qualified tenants. The Connector hears the need, makes the right introduction, and structures a simple agreement so that value shared becomes revenue earned.

Deliverables you can promise as a Connector: a vetted short list within forty-eight hours, a warm intro with context and expectations, and a follow-up report that tracks conversion. Trust grows when outcomes are visible.

Modern Examples

Zillow and Redfin: They connect buyers, sellers, and agents. They do not own homes. They own traffic and data flow.

BiggerPockets: A content and community platform that connects investors with knowledge and providers. It earns through memberships, sponsors, and partnerships.

CoStar Group: Holds a vast commercial data asset. By controlling information and access, it connects brokers and investors at scale.

These are large-scale proofs. At the personal level, a Connector can create meaningful recurring income through introductions, affiliates, and referral structures.

A thoughtful agent can build a six-figure side business by connecting contractors, mortgage lenders, insurance providers, and stagers, all under compliant and clear agreements.

Connector Framework

Value Engine: Relationships → Trust → Introductions → Revenue

Primary Assets: Network, credibility, access to data, and people

Monetization Models

- Referral agreements
- Sponsored communities
- Paid introductions
- Private network memberships

Growth Leverage: Digital platforms such as LinkedIn, private groups, newsletters, and community apps

Mindset Shift

Connectors do not push. They curate. They earn trust by putting outcomes first and by thinking long-term about every relationship.

A simple introduction can become a joint venture, a revenue share, or a seat at a larger table. The empire lives in plain sight, yet the power is invisible.

The Controller: Mastering Assets You Do Not Own

The Controller is the operator. This is the person who turns underperforming assets into performers. The building may belong to someone else. The results belong to the Controller.

The leverage is practical. A Controller can run ten units with the time and capital a buyer would sink into one. Risk sits on process rather than on debt, and process can be tuned in weeks rather than years. Efficiency becomes its own form of equity when repeated.

Controllers think like owners and work like systems engineers. They earn from management fees, revenue shares, and spreads created through better execution.

They learn fast, standardize what works, and scale through a repeatable process.

Imagine a property with weak occupancy, sloppy pricing, and uneven guest experience. A Controller steps in with clean workflows, smart pricing, sharp reporting, and a clear promise to the owner.

Revenue rises. Problems fall. Everyone wins.

Modern Examples

Airbnb hosts and management firms: Many of the most effective hosts do not own their listings. They use master lease arrangements, furnish with care, and run operations for a premium.

Sonder: Built a global brand on long-term control and short-term hospitality.

Vacasa: Scaled vacation rental management by focusing on control contracts rather than ownership.

WeWork: A complex story, yet it popularized the spread between long-term lease and short-term flexibility as a service.

Controllers win by tuning what others overlook. Pricing and positioning. Occupancy and experience. Process and measurement. When the system is sound, profit becomes predictable.

Controller Framework

Value Engine: Contract → Control → Optimization → Profit

Primary Assets: Processes, systems, people, and playbooks

Monetization Models

- Management fees based on flat terms or a percentage
- Revenue sharing agreements
- Master lease or control-based arbitrage
- Operational consulting contracts

Growth Leverage: Standardized operating systems, automation, training, and brand scale

Mindset Shift

Controllers accept a simple truth. Ownership often adds friction. Control often adds freedom. Skills compound with every property under care.

As the portfolio of controlled assets grows, cash flow becomes steadier and more forecastable. The Controller builds wealth through execution and through the reputation that follows consistent results.

Guardrails: cap fixed lease exposure by market, keep a ninety-day cash buffer for operations, and define stop loss rules for underperforming assets so you can exit without emotion.

The Creator: Owning the Digital Landscape

The Creator builds invisible assets that work while you sleep. These assets include websites, audiences, funnels, and platforms that pull attention in a steady stream and convert it into income.

Creator assets are digital properties. Websites, newsletters, deal hubs, local directories, and audience platforms behave like income real estate without roofs or repairs. When they capture attention, they capture deal flow, and deal flow can be monetized in many clean, low weight ways.

The arena is the attention economy, where visibility becomes value. Instead of holding land, the Creator holds digital real estate that attracts and monetizes traffic. Wealth grows through information leverage that scales without heavy capital.

Modern Examples

Luxury Presence and Agent Image – These firms create and license real estate websites for agents and brokerages, then earn recurring revenue through hosting, design, and search optimization.

BiggerPockets and Inman – These platforms turn trust and authority into subscriptions, sponsors, and affiliate income. It is a digital property that pays like a portfolio.

Niche websites – Solo operators build local home search portals or rental guides, then sell the leads to agents or property managers.

These platforms earn through advertising, data, and digital licensing. Think of it as rent collected from attention rather than from tenants.

Field exercise

One niche domain, ten pages that answer the top ten buyer or seller questions, one lead magnet, and one email sequence. Publish weekly, then add distribution before adding features.

Avoid the common trap of building first and promoting later. In digital real estate, distribution creates value faster than design.

Creator Framework

Value Engine: Attention → Trust → Conversion → Recurrence

Primary Assets: Websites, audiences, first-party data

Monetization Models

- Lead sales and licensing
- Affiliate partnerships
- Digital advertising and sponsorships
- Courses and subscription models

Growth Leverage: Search, social media, marketing automation, and artificial intelligence tools

Mindset Shift

Creators do not compete with agents or investors. They power them. By controlling visibility, they become gatekeepers of opportunity.

The properties are digital, yet the income is very real, recurring, and location independent. The Creator acts like a landlord whose best tenants are clicks that return repeatedly.

Signal You Are Ready to Scale

Your cost per subscriber is stable, your open rates stay healthy, and at least one monetization stream pays for content creation. Then replicate by market or by avatar, not by whim.

The Collaborator: Trading Skill for Equity

The Collaborator treats expertise as capital. Rather than working for a single payment, they structure agreements that continue to pay for as long as the value lasts.

This is expertise converted into participation. Instead of selling time once, Collaborators attach skill to outcomes and accept profit shares, advisory equity, or recurring compensation. As their portfolio of wins grows, their invitation list and pricing power grow with it.

They exchange rare skills in design, finance, construction, or marketing for equity or a share of profits in the projects they help to create.

Wealth here comes from skill leverage and from the judgment to choose the right partners.

Modern Examples

Architects and designers – Boutique studios sometimes accept a portion of equity in a development in place of all or part of their fees. The result feels like ownership level returns without taking on debt.

Property managers or contractors – Some teams accept a small share of profits in exchange for management or renovation work.

Advisors and consultants – Clear agreements convert advisory time into a continuing royalty on ongoing operations.

You can see this model even at scale. Large firms such as Related and Hines often invite outside specialists to participate based on performance rather than payroll.

Collaborator Framework

Value Engine: Expertise → Integration → Partnership → Equity

Primary Assets: Skill set, reputation, deep relationships, lived experience

Monetization Models

- Profit participation agreements
- Equity for service contracts
- Advisory shares or consulting royalties
- Co-development partnerships

Growth Leverage: Trusted partners, strong positioning, proven specialization

Mindset Shift

Collaborators live by a simple rule. Do the work once, get paid again and again. They do not sell hours.

They build residuals. Every project becomes a chance to accumulate invisible ownership without taking balance sheet risk.

Positioning tip: Publish three short case summaries that quantify outcomes. Results sell collaboration better than credentials.

Mixing Archetypes for Maximum Leverage

The strongest invisible investors rarely stay in one lane. They stack archetypes so that each one multiplies the others. A Controller becomes a Creator by running a lead platform that feeds the homes they operate.

A Connector becomes a Collaborator by trading key introductions for advisory shares. A Creator partners with Controllers so that audience traffic turns into managed revenue. Each layer compounds reach, trust, and cash flow.

Build a compound map. Draw four boxes for the archetypes and list one action this month that links each box to the next. Your first flywheel is one loop, not a labyrinth.

These roles are fluid on purpose. A Creator who shares useful content becomes a Connector. A Controller whose playbooks are sought after becomes a Collaborator. The strongest portfolios blend lanes so that each one feeds the next.

The Invisible Portfolio Framework

Treat the archetypes like asset classes. Instead of stocks and bonds, you allocate across relationships, systems, content, and expertise.

A sample mix might look like this

- 30% Connector income from referrals and partnerships
- 40% Controller income from management and operations
- 20% Creator income from digital platforms and lead systems
- 10% Collaborator income from equity and profit shares

A portfolio built this way becomes resilient and even antifragility. It can thrive through different market cycles because it earns from multiple streams that do not move in lockstep.

Rebalance quarterly. Shift 10% of your effort toward the archetype with the highest return on time last quarter and reduce the lowest. Portfolios grow when attention follows results.

Designing Your Archetype Strategy

Choose your dominant path with four questions.

- What comes most naturally to you: networking, systems, marketing, or expertise?
- What do people already pay you for?

- Which part of real estate do you enjoy most: finding deals, operating them, promoting them, or improving them?
- How can you monetize that value without ownership or heavy capital?

Your answers reveal the primary archetype and a clear entry point into invisible investing.

Decision rule: if two paths tie, pick the one that requires the fewest new tools and the fewest new relationships. Momentum compounds faster than reinvention.

When the model matches your nature, momentum feels inevitable. Start where you already have pull, then layer the next archetype only when the first one produces steady, measured results.

The Power of Alignment

Invisible investing does not step away from real estate. It steps into a role that fits you. When your wealth model matches your natural leverage, growth starts to feel inevitable.

Each of the four paths creates financial independence through a different kind of control. The best part? None of them requires a title.

Next, we will go deeper into the first archetype, the Connector, and turn relationships into recurring revenue in both online and offline channels. In the invisible economy, your network is not only your net worth. It is your cash flow system.

Common Pitfalls When You Start

- **Starting wide instead of narrow.**

  Build for one avatar and one outcome first.

- **Chasing tools over traction.**

  Make the offer work before you automate.

- **Measuring vanity instead of value.**

  Optimize for introductions, occupancy, or conversions, not likes.

Quick Start Plans by Archetype

- **Connector:** Launch a weekly email to a niche and sell three sponsor slots.
- **Controller:** Take over one underperforming unit and raise occupancy by ten percent.
- **Creator:** Publish ten pillar pages and one lead magnet.
- **Collaborator:** Convert one active client into a small profit share with clear metrics.

The Connector: Turning Relationships into Revenue

In every active market, there is someone who hears about the real deal first. Partners praise them. Operators text them. Investors' route updates through them. They rarely own the most property. They own the path between people, information, and opportunity. That is the Connector.

The New Power Brokers

The most valuable resource in real estate is not money, land, or even property. It is relationships. Decades ago, the wealthiest people in real estate were the ones who owned the most buildings.

Most markets run inside small circles of trust. Investors lean on familiar partners. Agents lean on familiar lenders. Operators lean on familiar contractors. The Connector widens the circle with speed and certainty, matching need to capacity in hours instead of weeks. The premium they earn is the premium for compression of time.

Today, the leaders are the ones who have the most access. Access to buyers. Access to data. Access to steady deal flow. This is the age of the Connector, the person or platform that makes opportunity move faster.

In a hyper-connected economy, being the bridge between people, services, and capital is often more profitable than being any one of those parts. The best part is that connection scales far faster than ownership.

What changed is the speed of matching. When information and intent move instantly, the value shifts to whoever reduces friction between need and solution.

A lender who can underwrite quickly, a contractor who can mobilize in days, and an agent who can surface verified buyers on short notice. The Connector compresses time to result, and the market pays a premium for that compression.

The Old Middleman and the New Connector

There was a time when middlemen were seen as a cost without value. Technology was supposed to remove them. That is not what happened. Technology created super connectors.

Platforms such as Zillow, CoStar, and LoopNet did not remove brokers. They became the broker layer. They own the pipeline, not the properties. They monetized the space between transactions, and that space turned out to be very valuable.

The modern Connector does not rely on inventory. The Connector monetizes flow, which includes leads, introductions, audiences, and trust.

Connectors make deals move.

The practical distinction is; middlemen clip a fee for passing along information. Connectors design, govern, and improve the pathway itself.

They standardize how introductions happen, track outcomes, and report value created. That is why they can charge retainers, sponsorships, and revenue shares rather than one-off finder's fees.

The modern Connector does not pass along scraps of information. They design the pathway, document expectations, and report outcomes. They are paid for enabling results, not for touching a file.

The Anatomy of a Connector Business

Every Connector business rests on three pillars.

- **Network capital** – the size and quality of your relationships
- **Trust equity** – your credibility within that network
- **Flow systems** – your ability to organize, automate, and monetize those relationships on a schedule

When these three parts align, your income becomes more predictable because opportunities begin to find you.

Think of it as pipeline math. If you maintain 200 relevant contacts, and 10% engage monthly, and 20% of those conversations convert to qualified introductions, you create four introductions per month. If your close rate on those introductions is 25% and your average revenue per closed intro is $1,000, the pipeline produces a steady income.

Improve any one variable and the system compounds.

Building Network Capital

In the old economy, networks were local. In the new economy, networks are digital ecosystems that stay active around the clock. A modern Connector might run any of the following.

- A community of ten thousand investors that lives on a social platform.
- A weekly newsletter that links agents and lenders to real inquiries.
- A private chat group where developers and capital sources meet.

These are not hobbies. They are income-producing ecosystems. The larger the network, the more leverage you earn, yet quality determines profitability.

Your goal as a Connector is not to meet everyone. It is to become indispensable to a focused group. When the network narrows, your relevance rises. Relevance is the engine of referrals.

1. Earning Trust Equity

Trust is the currency that converts connection into cash flow. You earn it through consistency and contribution. Share value freely. Make introductions without demand.

Show up with insight rather than a pitch. In every network, there are nodes, the people others rely on for clarity. They receive the first call when something must happen.

You aim to become that node. Once you are trusted, the market begins to route opportunities through you.

Track trust as behavior, not feeling. Signals include unsolicited inbound asks, repeat sponsors, and short response times to your messages.

If your average time to a meaningful reply is under 24 hours and your repeat sponsor rate is above 50%, you are compounding trust equity.

People remember the person who opened the right door at the right moment. One well timed introduction can echo for years, and that echo is what turns goodwill into durable income.

2. Creating Flow Systems

Without systems, networks slow down. The Connector builds flow infrastructure that turns social capital into orderly income.

- A customer relationship manager to track people and promises
- A scheduling link for fast introductions and short meetings
- Automation for reminders and follow-ups
- Simple monetization funnels for sponsors and referrals

Here is a clear example.

A marketing professional runs a local real estate newsletter that highlights top agents, lending experts, and home service providers.

The owner sells five monthly sponsorships at $500 each for a total of $2,500 per month in recurring revenue and rotates guest features for visibility.

The same platform creates referral income when introductions close. Valuable, light, and scalable, and built on trust.

Connector Economics and Offers

Price access by outcome, not audience size. Start with three rungs.

- Tier one: newsletter or group placement with a clear placement count and a conversion report.
- Tier two: warm introduction packages with a minimum qualified introduction count per month.
- Tier three: partner seat with co-branded events and shared pipelines.

Anchor pricing to the value at stake. If one closed client is worth $500 to a sponsor, a $500 monthly placement is a low-risk test.

Case Study: The BiggerPockets Model

To see the Connector at scale, look at BiggerPockets.

What began as an online forum grew into a content and community platform that connects millions of investors, service providers, and educators. BiggerPockets does not flip houses or lend money. It owns attention, and attention that turns into connection becomes the base of invisible investing.

The platform earns from memberships, sponsors, and advertising partnerships. The largest brands in real estate pay to access the network because the audience already trusts the platform.

Own the relationship, and others pay for access.

Case Study: CoStar and the Power of Data

CoStar Group is another masterclass in connection economics. It does not own buildings.

It owns the information about them. By collecting and curating data about who owns what, who leases what, and who is searching for what, it controls the flow of clarity.

That clarity becomes recurring subscription revenue for the serious players who must use it.

CoStar does not sell property. It sells insight.

Insight is an access product. Even if your "dataset" is a small market, you can publish verified lists, deal digests, and vendor scorecards that others rely on. When your information becomes reference grade, sponsors line up to be near it.

Case Study: Compass and Relationship Infrastructure

Compass did not rely only on a commission split or a sign. Its real innovation was the relationship infrastructure. The company built a system that tracks and amplifies the network power of agents.

The customer relationship manager keeps an agent top of mind through reminders, helpful outreach, and data insights. The result is a scaled Connector model across thousands of agents.

The product is not property. The product is people flow.

Replicate the principle at the micro scale. Equip your contributors with a simple playbook and shared templates for outreach, follow-up, and reporting. When many individuals follow one rhythm, the whole network compounds.

Micro Connectors: The Individual Edge

You can scale connection without debt, heavy capital, or inventory. What compounds is your reliability and your ability to route the next call to the next best fit.

You do not need millions of users or large funding to become a Connector. You need to spot a gap and fill it. Here are three practical models that any real estate professional can use.

Vendor ecosystem model.

Curate a network of lenders, inspectors, contractors, and stagers. Charge a modest marketing or sponsor fee to be featured in a private group, a site, or a live event.

Referral exchange model.

Create a transparent system where agents in different markets pay a set fee or a small percentage for introductions to buyers or investors.

Information marketplace model.

Launch a paid newsletter, a mastermind, or a series of events that brings dealmakers and specialists together. Monetize through access rather than ownership.

Each of these can begin part-time and grow into a six-figure recurring business within a year, depending on market fit and consistency.

Package the promise in one sentence and one metric. For example, "Two qualified introductions per week to active cash buyers in Ventura County" or "Five vendor bookings per month from homeowners planning to list in the next ninety days." Clear math converts faster than vague access.

Legal and Ethical Foundations

Transparency and compliance are essential for Connectors.

When you earn from introductions or referrals, you enter a regulated setting. Follow federal and state laws, including the (RESPA) Real Estate Settlement Procedures Act, which restricts unlicensed referral compensation in many contexts.

That does not mean you cannot monetize your work. It means you need the right structure.

- Use paid sponsorship or marketing agreements rather than unlicensed referral fees.
- Participate with the appropriate license when you refer clients

- Use written partnership contracts that define deliverables and reporting

Your currency is trust. Shortcuts destroy it. Integrity compounds it.

Decision map: if the payment is tied to a specific consumer transaction and you are unlicensed, avoid it. If the payment is for brand placement, content, or access to a professional audience you own, structure it as sponsorship.

When in doubt, insist on written disclosures and let the consumer choose among at least two options. Sunlight preserves trust.

The Digital Connector Toolkit

Operate like a professional by building a simple stack of tools.

1. **Customer relationship manager (CRM).**

   Tools like HubSpot, Pipedrive, or FollowUpBoss help you track every relationship, reminder, and follow-up.

2. **Email marketing platforms.**

   ConvertKit, Beehiiv, or Substack to turn your list into a broadcast channel.

3. **Scheduling and automation.**

   Calendly, Zapier, and Notion help streamline introductions and tasks.

4. **Community platform.**

   A private Circle space, Discord, or Facebook Group, where your network meets and engages.

5. **Analytics dashboard.**

   Track open rates, conversions, and introductions so you can quantify value.

When you can measure the performance of your network, you can scale it like any other business asset.

Scaling Connection

Once your systems are running, scale in three directions.

Vertical expansion

Deepen your reach in one niche, such as multifamily investors, luxury agents, or property technology founders.

Horizontal expansion

Add complementary sectors such as insurance, lending, or construction to your ecosystem.

Digital expansion

Use content and SEO to build audiences beyond your immediate geography. Think of a YouTube channel, podcast, or LinkedIn newsletter that attracts thousands of professionals who want in.

Each layer multiplies the value of your existing relationships. That is a compounding connection in action.

Guard against dilution. Add one new lane only after renewals exceed 80% and your average time to introduction is under 72 hours for the current lane. Scale what is smooth, not what is shiny.

The Compound Effect of Introductions

A single introduction can change a career. The effect of introductions grows over time because each new relationship multiplies the reach of your network.

If every trusted contact introduces you to two others, and you do the same, your influence can double with each round.

It is not a straight line. It is closer to a chain reaction. Every new connection increases the value of the ones that came before.

The Invisible Asset: Reputation

Reputation is a form of capital. It's the only asset that grows stronger the more you share it.

In traditional investing, you compound money. In invisible investing, you compound credibility.

The stronger your reputation, the faster opportunities find you. This is why the best Connectors are generous with information, introductions, and time.

Visibility creates velocity, and velocity builds wealth.

Reputation also defends pricing. Publish case notes and anonymized metrics so sponsors see the engine behind the fee. When value is documented, discount pressure fades.

Monetizing Access

When your network has momentum, you can monetize in more than one way.

- **Sponsorships**. Sell placement in your newsletter or community.
- **Partnerships**. Charge for curated introductions or co-branded events.
- **Memberships**. Offer a private mastermind or an investor group for a monthly fee.
- **Education**. Teach strategic networking through courses, workshops, or advisory work.

Each stream reinforces your position at the center of the ecosystem. As relationships compound, your income can grow without linear effort.

Control churn with success plans. For each sponsor or member, document the one result that would make renewal automatic, then align programming to that result. Retention is the true price power.

Sample Template and Script

Warm intro template: "Pat, meet Jordan. Pat helps first-time investors structure creative debt in Ventura. Jordan runs four duplex rehabs a year and is exploring longer-term fixed-rate options. Opt in here if helpful, opt out if timing is wrong. I will circle back in two weeks to record outcomes."

Sponsor outreach note: "We have two placements left next month in a newsletter that delivers forty to sixty qualified introductions across Ventura County. One closed client usually covers six to ten months of placement. Would you like the media kit and a sample issue?"

The Connector Golden Rule

Connector wealth rests on a simple paradox. You earn more when you stop trying to extract from every interaction. Shift your goal from transaction profit to relationship profit, and the market rewards you with scale.

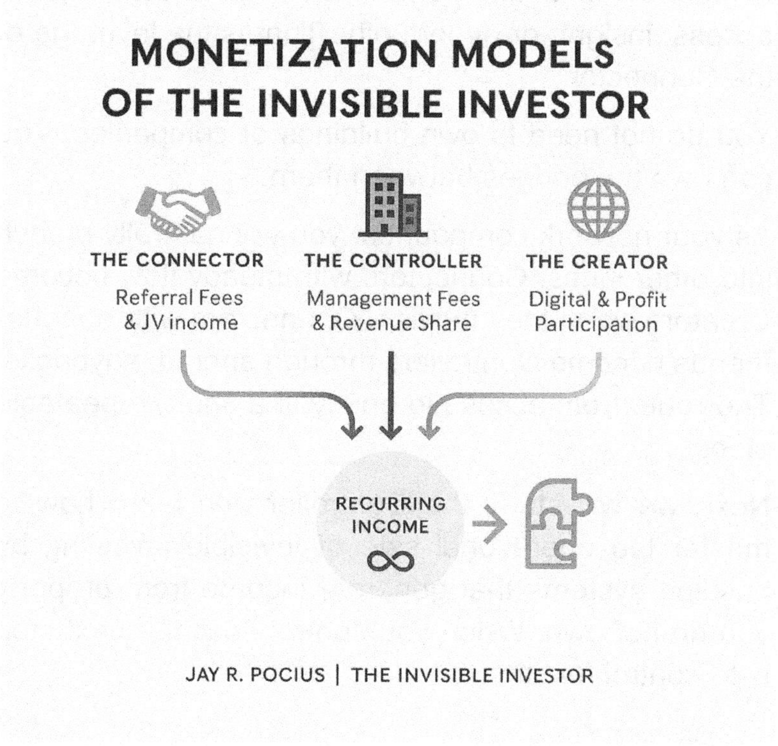

Your network becomes your asset. Your reputation becomes your brand. Your introductions become your income. At that point, you are no longer a participant.

You are an essential part of the market.

Guardrail: decline any introduction that would trade short-term cash for long-term trust. Keep a written list of no-go categories and stick to it. The deals you turn down signal what your brand protects.

Conclusion: Connection as Control

Control does not always mean a contract. Sometimes it means being the person who holds the keys to access, insight, or opportunity. That is the leverage of the Connector.

You do not need to own buildings or companies. You can own the bridges between them.

As your network compounds, you will naturally branch into other lanes. Connectors with steady flow become Creators when they publish. Connectors with operator friends become Controllers through shared playbooks. The route from access to equity is a short, repeatable step.

Next, we will study the Controller and learn how to master the operational side of invisible investing by building systems that generate income from property you do not own. When you control flow, the next step is to control function.

The Controller: Mastering Assets You Do Not Own

Controllers operate behind the scenes and often out earn the owners they serve. Their skill is turning underperforming or unmanaged assets into consistent cash flow by installing pricing discipline, process clarity, and clean reporting. In short-term rentals, corporate housing, flex stay, and long-term portfolios, Controllers bring order that owners rarely have time to build.

Many landlords are passive by necessity, not by design. Controllers bridge that gap with master leases, operating agreements, or management contracts that hand them the wheel without loading them with debt. The result is real leverage. A Controller can operate ten doors with the same time and capital that a traditional investor would sink into one. Efficiency becomes equity when it repeats across many units.

The Operator Advantage

Every property tells a story, yet the owner is not always the author. Across markets, operators are the ones who transform buildings into brands, turn space into income, and manage the path from bricks to the balance sheet.

These operators are Controllers, individuals, or companies that generate revenue by running real estate owned by others. They do not hold the deed. They hold the keys to consistent performance.

The Controller's advantage lies in leverage. Owners are tied to capital. Controllers are tied to competence. They scale through execution rather than acquisition.

If the Connector builds bridges, the Controller is the engineer who keeps traffic flowing and earns a toll on every car that crosses.

At the core is unit economics. Each door has a revenue ceiling and a cost floor. The Controller narrows the gap between them through pricing, positioning, process, and people. Improve the four P's and the spread appears without buying a new asset.

Think of the Controller as the profit engineer. They move the revenue ceiling with dynamic rate strategy, they lower the cost floor with tighter labor and vendor standards, and they compress the gap with service design that prevents rework. When this loop is documented, each new unit becomes faster to stabilize. That is how Controllers scale through execution rather than acquisition.

The Rise of the Control Model

The move from ownership to operation began in hospitality. Most people don't realize that companies like Marriott, Hilton, and Hyatt own less than 1% of the hotels that bear their names.

Many properties are managed or franchised under agreements that grant control over brand, pricing, and guest experience without owning the real estate.

That asset-light strategy sits at the center of modern invisible investing. It is how firms such as Airbnb, Sonder, and Vacasa scaled without billions in property acquisitions.

- **Airbnb** – Built a trillion-dollar brand around inventory it does not own. Hosts take the ownership risk while Airbnb controls the marketplace and the reputation layer.
- **Sonder**. Signs long-term leases on apartments and offers them as designer short-term stays, earning a margin between a fixed rent and dynamic nightly rates.
- **Vacasa**. Manages vacation homes for owners and collects fees and profit shares from performance.
- **WeWork**. A complex case that popularized the idea of space arbitrage, where a long lease becomes flexible workspace at a premium.

These examples share one pattern. Ownership supplies the box. Control designs what happens inside the box. When brand, pricing, and guest experience are governed by a repeatable system, the Controller captures more of the economics than title alone would allow, and does so with less risk and more agility.

The Mechanics of Control

Control first asks a single question. How can I influence cash flow without buying the asset? Three frameworks make that possible.

1. Master Lease Model

A master lease is a long-term rental agreement between an operator and an owner. You lease the property, gain the right to sublet or manage, and pay the owner a fixed amount each month.

If you can generate more revenue than the lease cost, the difference is your profit.

Example. You lease a four-unit property for $6,000 each month. You furnish the homes and rent them as short-term corporate housing for $10,000 each month.

After $1,500 in expenses, your net is $2,500 per month, or $30,000 per year, on a property you do not own.

No mortgage. No property tax. This model works in residential, commercial, and hospitality settings where flexibility and experience add value.

2. Management Contract Model

In this model, you operate a property for an owner for a percentage of revenue (usually 10–25%) or a flat monthly fee. You handle bookings, marketing, maintenance, and guest care. The owner receives income without effort. You receive recurring cash flow.

Example. You manage ten short-term rental homes that gross $3,000 each month on average. At a 20% fee, your income is $6,000 each month without leases or ownership risk.

Lean, predictable, and scalable.

3. Revenue Share Partnership Model

This hybrid approach replaces a fixed lease or fee with a profit split. You and the owner share revenue based on performance targets so that both parties benefit from improvement.

Example. You operate a boutique property for a 50/50 split after expenses. Gross income rises from $8,000 each month to $12,000 after you optimize pricing and design.

You both net more, and you created equity-like returns without buying the building.

Align the split to the lever you control. If you control rate and occupancy, share above a baseline net operating income, so the owner always feels protected. If you control channel mix and direct bookings, add a small kicker when platform fees decline. Incentives guide behavior.

Beyond structure, the Controller's edge comes from five controllable levers. Channel mix that favors direct bookings over high-fee platforms. Pricing rules that combine seasonality, lead time, weekday patterns, and local events. Turnover operations with checklists that cut variance and protect reviews. Owner communication that sets expectations with a simple weekly scorecard. Vendor economics that lock in response time and quality tiers. When these levers are measured weekly, drift disappears and margin shows up.

The Controller Mindset

Controllers view inefficiency as an opportunity. Many owners do not have the time, skill, or systems to maximize revenue. Controllers step in, take responsibility, and turn chaos into cash flow.

Their value is execution intelligence. They spot performance leaks in occupancy, pricing, or guest experience and fix them profitably. They do not speculate on appreciation. They engineer income.

Ownership is a bet. Control is a business.

Daily exercise: forecast tomorrow, act today, review yesterday. Forecast expected occupancy and rate by channel, act on pricing and tasks, then review variances each morning. Small daily course corrections create large monthly deltas.

Case Study: Sonder and the Design of Control

Sonder began with a simple idea in 2014. Lease apartments, redesign them with a consistent look, and offer them as stylish short-term stays.

The company did not buy buildings. It reimagined them. With a blend of hospitality design and reliable standards, Sonder reached thousands of units around the world.

Agreements range from master leases to revenue shares, depending on the market. The leverage point is brand and systems.

Owners want the prestige and efficiency that Sonder brings. Sonder wants a predictable supply and control over the guest experience. The lesson is simple.

In a control-based model, execution replaces equity.

Case Study: Vacasa and the Management Machine

Vacasa chose a different path. Rather than leasing, it built on pure management contracts. By offering full-service operations that include marketing, cleaning, maintenance, and dynamic pricing, it convinced owners to outsource.

The secret was automation. Proprietary software-priced homes in real time based on demand in the same way airlines price seats. That drove occupancy and revenue together.

Owners gained hands-off income. Vacasa built a valuable business by managing properties it did not own.

Lesson for small firms: invest early in rate discipline. Even a simple dynamic rule based on weekday, lead-time, and event calendars can lift revenue ten to fifteen percent over static pricing.

Case Study: Marriott Homes & Villas

Even the legacy brands embrace the control model. Marriott launched Homes & Villas by Marriott International in 2019 to compete in the luxury home-rental space.

But Marriott didn't buy properties.

Marriott provided brand trust, a booking base, and distribution. Operators provided homes and services. Revenue was shared. The company captured a share of the short-term rental market without capital risk.

Controllers do not fight ownership. They enhance it.

Most owners do not buy a system. They buy relief. Frame the offer in outcomes the owner already wants. Fewer calls, clearer reporting, better reviews, and predictable deposits. Replace long proposals with an option table, a fixed lease for stability, a management fee for simplicity, and a performance split for aligned upside. Choice lowers friction and makes yes feel safe.

How to Negotiate Control

To build a Controller business, learn to negotiate agreements where both sides win. Use this sequence.

1. **Identify Underperforming Properties**

   Look for listings with low occupancy, poor reviews, or inefficient pricing. These are opportunities to add value.

2. **Research the Numbers**

   Use tools like AirDNA, PriceLabs, or Mashvisor to estimate market demand, seasonal rates, and potential revenue.

3. **Pitch Performance, Not Potential**

   Owners don't care about your enthusiasm; they care about predictability. Present a clear plan showing how your management or leasing model will improve income and reduce hassle.

4. **Offer Multiple Options**

   Give owners flexibility:

   - Fixed lease (stable rent).
   - Management (percentage of gross).
   - Revenue share (aligned upside).
   - Choice builds trust.

5. **Protect Yourself Contractually**

   Use clear agreements that define:

   - Duration and termination terms.
   - Revenue splits and reporting methods.
   - Maintenance responsibilities.
   - Insurance and liability coverage.

6. **Deliver Transparency**

   Provide owners with dashboards or regular reports showing occupancy, pricing, and maintenance status.
   Visibility builds longevity.

30, 60, 90 Day Turnaround Plan

Day 1 to 30: Stabilize and see. Fix cleaning and response times, install a channel manager, set a simple dynamic pricing rule, and repair the top five guest complaints.

Day 31 to 60: Optimize and document. Tune photos and copy, launch a direct booking page, standardize owner reporting, and test a small upsell menu.

Day 61 to 90: Scale and decide. Add distribution partners, negotiate vendor rates, set monthly targets, and decide whether to extend, expand, or exit.

The Power of Systems

Controllers do not scale by working more hours. They scale by standardizing and automating the work that repeats.

Core system components include the following.

- **Channel Manager:** Syncs listings across Airbnb, VRBO, Booking.com, etc. (e.g., Hostaway, Guesty).
- **Dynamic Pricing Tools:** Adjust nightly rates automatically based on demand. (PriceLabs, Wheelhouse).
- **Task Management:** Automate cleaning and maintenance schedules (Turno, Breezeway).
- **Communication Automation:** AI chatbots for guest messages, FAQs, and review requests.
- **Financial Dashboards:** Track revenue, expenses, and owner payouts in real-time.

These tools turn operational chaos into control, and once you have control, scale becomes inevitable.

Scaling a Controller Business

Grow vertically or horizontally once your playbook is proven.

Vertical Growth – Deep Control in One Market

Specialize in one region or one asset type, such as coastal vacation homes or downtown apartments.

Build brand reputation and owner referrals, and local partnerships.

Horizontal growth – Multiple Markets, Same Systems

Once your systems are proven, expand to new cities. Hire local contractors for operations, keep marketing and pricing centralized.

Brand licensing – The Controller Multiplied

Package your systems and license them to other operators under your brand. Earn royalties or advisory fees. This is how Airbnb Superhosts, boutique property managers, and hotel brands scale globally.

Risk Management

Control doesn't mean immunity from risk; it means managing it intelligently.

Key risks and how to mitigate them:

- **Vacancy risk on leased property** – Keep flexible terms and use dynamic pricing to maintain occupancy
- **Legal risk** – Check zoning and permits, and carry proper business insurance.
- **Operational risk** – Standardize processes, vet vendors, and maintain clear owner communication.
- **Reputation risk** – Manage reviews aggressively; one bad experience can impact dozens of future bookings.

Control does not erase risk; it moves where you manage it. Create preset exits and pauses. If occupancy drops below a threshold for two consecutive cycles, trigger a pricing audit and channel shift. If review averages slip, halt expansion and fix root causes before adding doors. If a city tightens rules, pivot inventory mix toward mid-term stays. A simple rule set turns surprises into play calls instead of panic.

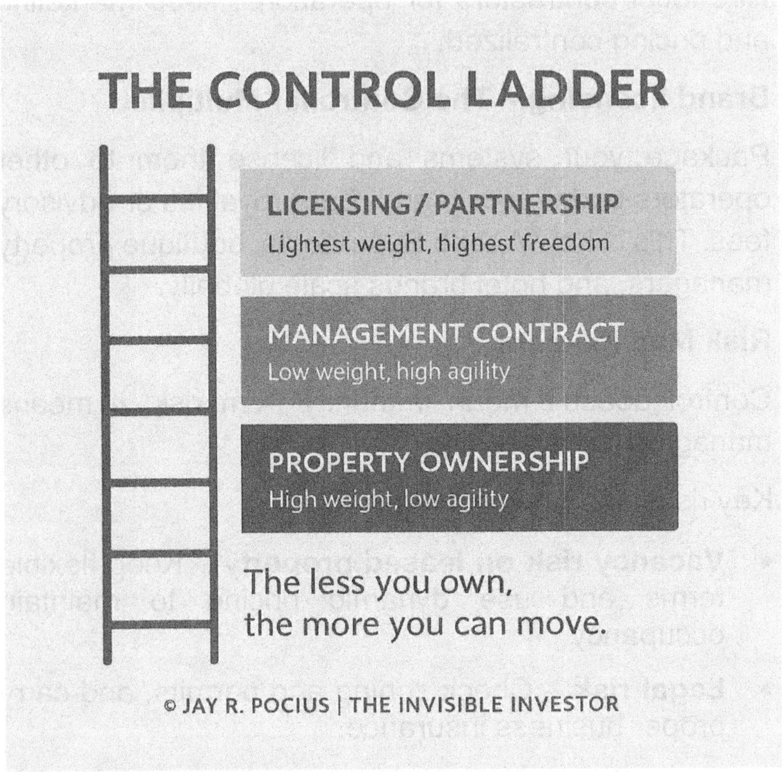

Why Controllers Win

Controllers win because they sit at the meeting point of efficiency and scale. They

- Build recurring income without heavy capital.
- Pivot quickly when markets change.

- Grow through systems instead of financing.
- Earn trust by delivering results rather than promises.

While ownership ties up money. Control frees it, and freedom compounds.

The Controller Framework

Core Concept	**Description**
Leverage Point	Operational control over someone else's asset
Key Resource	Systems, contracts, relationships
Primary Income	Management fees, profit shares, and lease spreads
Scaling Tool	Automation, delegation, and brand reputation
Risk Exposure	Low capital, moderate operational
Freedom Factor	High — minimal debt, high adaptability

The Invisible Advantage

Ownership creates a straight line. Each new building requires new capital. Control creates a curve. Each new agreement multiplies the value of your playbook.

Controllers build businesses rather than collections. They do not wait for appreciation. They create value through daily execution.

Exit protocols matter. Define three reasons you will exit a lease or contract, a handover checklist for owners, and a communication plan that protects reputation. Leaving well is part of scaling well.

Conclusion: The Power of Performance

The Controller is the heart of invisible investing. Wealth comes from execution rather than ownership. They prove freedom does not come from collecting deeds; it comes from mastering operations.

There will always be owners who have assets yet lack systems. There will always be Controllers who have systems yet do not need assets.

Fieldwork: Select one underperforming unit or service line and run the 90-day turnaround. Document before and after revenue, review score, and owner sentiment. That case study becomes your new lead engine.

In a control-based business, the real asset is the playbook. Agreements come and go, but a playbook that reliably turns space into spread compounds every time you run it.

Looking Ahead

Next, we will explore the Creator and see how digital property has become a powerful new frontier. Because in the invisible economy, whoever controls attention controls everything.

The Creator: Building Digital Real Estate

Creators are real estate developers who build with attention instead of concrete. Their properties are digital, websites, lead funnels, newsletters, social platforms, directories, and marketplaces. These assets may not live on a balance sheet, yet they often produce returns that rival or exceed rentals when measured per dollar and per hour.

What separates a Creator from a casual marketer is repeatability. The asset is not one video or one page. It is a system that captures attention at a known cost, converts it at a known rate, and retains it with a known cadence. When these numbers are stable, the digital property throws predictable cash the way a well-run building throws rent.

The New Frontier of Property

A generation ago, real estate meant land, buildings, and brick. Today, it also means pixels, pages, and platforms. When someone searches “homes for sale in Ventura”, the first website they see is digital property.

It earns traffic, generates leads, and converts attention into money, just like a physical building converts tenants into rent.

That is the domain of the Creator, the invisible investor who builds, owns, or licenses digital infrastructure that powers the real estate economy.

Creators do not flip houses; they flip attention. They design, rank, and monetize the online spaces where buyers, sellers, and investors meet.

Attention is not vanity. It is inventory. When a page ranks for a local intent query, it holds shelf space that agents, lenders, and vendors are willing to rent. When a newsletter lands at the same time every week with useful local data, it becomes a habit, and habits are the strongest kind of demand. Creators do not chase algorithms; they design habits.

What distinguishes a Creator from a casual marketer is repeatable capture. The asset is not one post or one page; it is a system that predictably acquires attention, and converts and retains it at a known cost.

From Dirt to Data

Real estate has always been about location. In the digital era, Google is the new geography. Where a site ranks on a search results page is no different from where a store sits on Main Street.

Top placement equals premium rent. If a physical billboard can command thousands per month for visibility, a high-ranking web page that drives the same or more exposure can do the same.

Creators understand that traffic is the new footfall, and search engine optimization is the new zoning code. They treat keywords like parcels, domains like buildings, and backlinks like roads connecting neighborhoods. Their portfolios are not made of street addresses. They are made of URLs.

Why Digital Real Estate Matters

More than ninety percent of real estate journeys begin online. That means whoever controls digital discovery controls the deal flow.

Owning a website, a video channel, or an email list that ranks high and reaches wide is like owning an endless pipeline of buyers, sellers, and investors.

These pipelines can be rented, sold, licensed, or automated.

Digital real estate produces recurring revenue through four main streams.

- **Leads** — sold or referred to agents, lenders, or vendors.
- **Ads & Sponsorships** — local companies paying for visibility.
- **Courses & Memberships** — turning knowledge into subscription income.
- **Affiliate Deals** — earning a share of products or services sold.

Map your unit economics before you write a word. Define a qualified lead, price it based on partner value, and set a minimum monthly delivery. If the average agent earns six thousand per closed side and converts one in twenty exclusive leads, a qualified lead is worth three hundred. Improve conversion with education and prescreening, and the value doubles. When you know these numbers, content has a clear job and sponsors see a clear return.

And unlike physical property, digital assets do not require down payments, appraisals, or tenants. They require strategy, creativity, and consistency.

Price your pipeline with simple math.

If the average agent earns $6,000 per closed side and converts 1 in 20 exclusive leads, a qualified lead is worth $300 pre-close ($6,000 ÷ 20).

If your audience warms leads so conversion improves to 1 in 10, that value doubles to $600. Set guaranteed lead minimums and clear refund terms to keep incentives aligned.

The Hidden Empire Companies Built on Digital Land

To see the power of this model, look at firms that already operate at a global scale.

1. Zillow

Zillow does not sell houses. It sells visibility to those who do. By ranking at the top of home-related search queries, it controls more digital real estate than any brokerage could hold physically. Its product is traffic, and its tenants are agents who pay for leads and exposure.

2. CoStar Group

CoStar built its empire by mapping and monetizing commercial property data. Its “parcels” are data sets, and its “buildings” are information platforms such as LoopNet, Apartments.com, and Homes.com. Brokers and developers effectively rent space on these platforms to reach clients.

3. BiggerPockets.

Beginning as a discussion forum, BiggerPockets grew into a content and community ecosystem with millions of users. It sells education, advertising, and partnerships built on digital trust.

4. Agent Image and Luxury Presence.

These firms design and host websites for brokerages and agents, charging monthly fees for maintenance, SEO, and lead capture. They build the subdivisions of digital land and collect rent through subscriptions.

Each of these companies proves the same truth. Digital control produces tangible wealth that can be more stable and more scalable than owning physical property.

The playbook is portable. You do not need a national scale; you need a durable local advantage: unique data, local relationships, and consistent publishing cadence. When your site becomes the fastest, most accurate source for a micro market, partners line up to "rent" your reach.

How to Build Digital Real Estate from Scratch

You do not need venture capital or a coding degree to become a Creator. You need a strategy, a niche, and a system. Here is the playbook.

Step 1 – Choose Your Digital Location

Pick a niche or market where you can dominate visibility, such as Ventura beachfront homes, Denver short-term rentals, or commercial spaces near airports. Narrow focus beats broad exposure.

Validate with three signals: underserved content (few high-quality guides), high advertiser value (cost per click above five dollars), and partner readiness (three or more local pros willing to sponsor day one). If two of three are present, proceed.

Step 2 – Acquire Your Domain

Secure a memorable, keyword-rich address, such as Corporatebusinessrental.com or InvestmentHomes.com.

Prefer short, readable, brand-able names. Avoid hyphens. Lock matching social handles and a simple email domain for trust.

Step 3 – Content & Design

Create articles, videos, listings, or guides that attract your audience. Good design is curb appeal. Strong SEO is foot traffic.

Publish a hub and spoke architecture. One pillar page per neighborhood with school info, commute times, price ranges, and three embedded videos.

Spokes include examples like “best realtor in NY,” “flip a house fast,” and “how to buy in this zip.” Add comparison pages that answer the exact debate locals have, such as “Midtown versus East End.”

Use a simple publishing rhythm. One pillar page each week, two support pieces that link back, one lead magnet per month, and one nurture email every seven days. Add one distribution lane at a time, search first, then a single social channel, then partnerships. Depth beats width. Consistency beats bursts.

Step 4 – Monetize the Traffic

Decide early how you will earn. It can be done either by

- Selling leads to agents or lenders.
- Offering sponsorship spots to vendors.
- Collecting affiliate commissions for insurance, moving, or staging.
- Building an email list for future digital launches.

Set a clear monetization ladder: free content for reach, email newsletter for nurture, sponsor placements for cash flow, exclusive lead packages for premium partners, and premium guides or data dashboards for recurring revenue. Move the audience up the ladder month by month.

Step 5 – Automate the Management

Use writing assistants, CRM automations, and analytics dashboards. Your site becomes a round-the-clock property manager that collects rent in the form of clicks.

Minimum stack: WordPress or Webflow, privacy-compliant analytics, tag manager, form capture into a CRM, and a weekly content calendar. Add structured data markup for listings, reviews, and FAQs to raise click-through and eligibility for rich results.

Step 6 – Scale Horizontally

Once one site ranks, replicate the model across nearby markets or related topics. Just like property developers, Creators replicate blueprints, not buildings.

Clone only what is working. Export your top twenty pages, their internal links, and their conversion elements. Use the same template in the next market and localize the data. This reduces spin-up time to weeks, not months.

Cloning works best when the blueprint is documented. Save your top performing page layout, internal link blocks, calls to action, and email sequence as a reusable kit. When you enter a new market, swap only the local data and media. This keeps creation light, protects quality, and shortens the path to rank and revenue.

Case Study: CityLiving Network

Imagine a small team that launches a series of hyperlocal lifestyle sites, CityLivingVentura.com, CityLivingSantaBarbara.com, and CityLivingOxnard.com.

Each site features neighborhood guides, event calendars, and listings powered by IDX feeds. The team monetizes by selling advertising slots to local mortgage lenders, restaurants, and service providers for $300 to $500 per month each.

After ranking on Google, the portfolio generates 20 to 30 qualified buyer leads per site each month. Those leads are sold to agents for $50 to $100 each.

Within 18 months, the portfolio earns $15,000 in recurring monthly revenue. No ownership. No leases. Only digital land that appreciates in visibility. That is invisible investing scaled through creativity rather than capital.

Add discipline, and the numbers improve.

If each site also captures 2000 email subscribers with a 5% percent monthly click to lead rate, that is 100 additional leads per month at near zero incremental cost. With basic drip sequences and two educational webinars per quarter, conversion rates rise without buying more traffic.

Digital Real Estate versus Physical Real Estate

Metric	Physical	Digital
Entry Cost	High (down payment, loan)	Low (domain + hosting)
Maintenance	Ongoing, physical	Minimal, automated
Appreciation	Market-driven	Performance-driven
Liquidity	Slow	Instant (sell, redirect, or license)

Metric	Physical	Digital
Risk	Local	Global diversification
Leverage	Financial	Technological

Owning a rental house might net $500 per month. A single well-ranked website can produce the same or more with very little overhead.

Framework: The Digital Asset Cycle

Build → Rank → Rent → Replicate.

- **Build**: Create a site or channel targeted to high-value search terms.
- **Rank**: Use SEO, social distribution, and backlinks to earn organic visibility.
- **Rent**: Monetize via ads, leads, or partnerships.
- **Replicate**: Use the same blueprint in a new market.

Each cycle compounds faster than the last because reputation, backlinks, and data carry over. Just as equity compounds in physical real estate, authority compounds in digital.

Use quarterly "renovations." Refresh top pages with new data, add internal links from new content, and insert a stronger call to action. Small updates sustain rankings and improve conversion.

Diversifying a Digital Portfolio

Creators rarely stop at one platform. They expand into an ecosystem.

- **Websites** — SEO and content marketing.
- **Email Lists** — Nurture and conversion.
- **Social Channels** — Awareness and traffic generation.
- **Courses / Communities** — Deep engagement and recurring subscriptions.

Together, these assets form a Digital Portfolio that behaves like a property portfolio. It is diversified, cash flowing, and saleable.

Score each asset monthly on three factors: audience size, trust metrics such as open rate and watch time, and monetization per thousand audience. Invest where the score is rising. Sunset what lags to avoid bloat.

Digital Equity: Valuing the Invisible

A website with steady traffic and revenue can be valued much like a business. Typical multiples range from thirty to fifty times monthly net profit.

A site that earns $2,000 per month might sell for $60,000 to $100,000, similar to the profit of flipping a small property, but without the capital or the risk.

Creators can exit by selling websites on established marketplaces or by selling directly to brokerages that want digital leads. Digital equity is both liquid and exponential.

Prepare for sale six months in advance. Clean up dependencies, document processes, shift revenue to recurring where possible, and reduce reliance on any one traffic source below 50%. Buyers pay for predictability.

Automation and AI Scaling the Invisible Workforce

Modern tools have increased the power of the Creator model.

- **Content**: AI tools generate articles, captions, and scripts at scale.
- **Analytics**: Predictive algorithms forecast search trends and traffic potential.
- **Chatbots**: Handle inbound leads or inquiries 24/7.
- **Design**: No-code platforms (Webflow, Wix Studio) reduce production time dramatically.

With the right stack, one Creator can manage what used to require a full agency. Automation turns skill into infrastructure.

However, automation multiplies output, but trust drives renewal. Add three simple guardrails to keep quality in check. Human edit anything that carries numbers or legal nuance. Disclose sponsors and affiliates in plain language. Refresh high traffic pages quarterly with new data and better answers to the same questions. These small practices protect reputation and keep rankings stable.

Common Monetization Models

There are five common revenue streams.

- **Lead licensing:** Sell exclusive or shared leads to agents and lenders through recurring contracts with minimum lead counts.
- **Advertising and sponsorship:** Offer banner space, featured listings, or co-branded content, which is similar to renting storefronts along your digital street.
- **Affiliate revenue:** Promote complementary products such as moving services, staging, digital products, or insurance, and earn commissions.
- **Education and digital products:** Package your process into mini courses or consulting services for agents and small businesses.
- **Membership communities:** Create local investors or homeowner groups with premium tiers for data and perks.

These streams can run concurrently, much like a mixed-use building with retail, office, and residential tenants.

Avoid channel conflict. If you sell exclusive leads to one broker, restrict competing brokers to the same page. If you run memberships, give sponsors clear placement rules. Consistency preserves renewals.

Creators who win long term build a portfolio, not a pile. Treat every site, list, and channel like a tenant in a mixed-use project. If one tenant slows, another covers the note. If one channel spikes, use that surplus to improve the others. Portfolio thinking smooths cash flow and makes the whole system more valuable at exit.

Brand as Leverage

Digital real estate appreciates fastest when it is attached to a recognizable brand. Once your audience trusts your name, each new product, site, or partnership inherits that trust.

That is why top influencers, content creators, and forward-looking brokerages now act like media companies. They control perception. Perception drives demand. The brand becomes an asset layer that raises the rental value of every digital property underneath it.

Case Study: BiggerPockets Pro

The paid membership tier at BiggerPockets offers a clear lesson in brand leverage. Members pay monthly for calculators, tools, and exclusive content.

Because the brand already controls the community, converting free users into paying subscribers is nearly frictionless. Their content compounds, their audience compounds, and their revenue compounds. The result is a triple flywheel of invisible equity.

Your micro version can be a $5 per month local data letter that publishes price per square foot trends, days on market by zip, and three fast takes on lending rules.

If one hundred locals subscribe, you have a baseline recurring engine that feeds every other product.

Legal and Ethical Considerations

As with physical real estate, ethics define longevity. Creators must be transparent in data use, advertising disclosure, and affiliate relationships.

- Always obtain permission before sharing leads.
- Disclose paid partnerships.
- Respect privacy and opt-out laws (CAN SPAM Act, GDPR, etc.).

Integrity is not only moral. It is algorithmic. Search engines reward transparency and penalize manipulation. Long-term wealth in digital property depends on trust, not tricks.

Scaling Beyond Yourself

When digital cash flow becomes consistent, the next move is delegation. Build a micro team.

- SEO specialist for growth.
- Virtual assistant for posting and outreach.
- Sales partner for lead management.
- Content editor to maintain quality.

Your role shifts from creator to editor-in-chief, who directs a portfolio of digital properties that work while you sleep.

That is when invisible income becomes true freedom.

Framework: The Creator Equation

Visibility × Trust × Monetization = Digital Equity

- Visibility brings traffic.
- Trust converts visitors.
- Monetization captures value.

Multiply all three, and you build assets that pay like properties and move like software.

If any factor is zero, equity is zero. Protect trust above all. Remove low-quality sponsors, correct errors publicly, and answer reader questions quickly.

Exit without Entry

Creators can sell or license their digital assets, sometimes for more than investors earn selling physical real estate.

Options include:

- **Asset sale** – where you transfer the website, content, and data.
- **Licensing agreement** – where others use your brand or system for royalties.
- **Joint venture** – where you partner with brokerages or lenders for exclusive access deals.

In each case, you are exiting an investment that never required a traditional entry. You built from information rather than infrastructure.

The Invisible Developer

The Creator is a developer of ideas. They build intangible structures made of words, pixels, and automation, and those structures produce tangible results.

Just like physical developers, Creators profit most when they design for scale. Each digital asset becomes a new building block in a larger ecosystem.

Link them together, and you no longer own individual websites. You own attention corridors.

Attention corridors are the sequence from search to article to lead magnet to call to action to consult. Map yours visually and remove every unnecessary click. Friction costs revenue.

Conclusion: Building the Future Skyline

In the old world, city skylines measured success. In the new world, search results pages do. Those who control the top positions own the view and the revenue that comes with it.

The Creator represents the most scalable path in invisible investing. There is no ceiling, no border, and no limit on replication.

When you build digital real estate, you do not simply profit from property. You redefine it. You prove that wealth does not come from ownership of matter, but from mastery of meaning.

In the next chapter, we will explore the Collaborator, the professional who turns expertise into equity by trading skill for partnership rather than payment.

Once you can control systems and visibility, the final step is learning how to share ownership without risk.

In the skyline of the modern market, search results pages and inboxes are the view that matters. Own that view, and you own the flow that follows. Digital properties move like software and pay like rentals when the system behind them is sound.

The Collaborator: Trading Skills for Equity

The Collaborator operates where expertise meets leverage. Designers who reshape demand, contractors who de risk execution, marketers who manufacture pipeline, consultants who engineer strategy, and lenders who unlock capital, all convert specialized skill into long-term participation. Their contribution is not always financial, yet it is foundational, and that is why they earn like owners without holding title.

The Shift from Paychecks to Profit Shares

Every industry reaches a moment when expertise is worth more than cash. In real estate, that moment is here. For decades, professionals such as contractors, designers, brokers, lenders, and marketers have been treated as vendors.

They get paid once, then watch the asset they improved continue to produce income for someone else. The Collaborator changes that. Instead of exchanging time for a fee, they exchange value for value.

They trade specialized skills for a percentage of the deal, turning short-term effort into long-term participation. This is the model that built Silicon Valley, where advisors often accept stock options rather than consulting checks.

Now it is transforming real estate.

The Core Idea Equity through Expertise

Equity is not only for investors with cash. It is for anyone who creates measurable value. When a contractor upgrades a multifamily property and rents rise by 25%, they have increased equity.

When a designer stages and rebrands a boutique hotel and bookings double, they have created equity. When a lender structures creative financing that saves a deal, they preserve equity.

The difference is whether they get paid once or paid forever. Collaborators understand that knowledge is capital. When it is leveraged correctly, it compounds like money.

The modern shift is simple, stop billing for hours and start billing for impact. Advisory roles, performance participation, and fractional equity turn outcomes into annuities. A rebrand that lifts rate, a pricing system that lifts occupancy or a capital stack that makes a deal possible, each is a value injection that persists after the work is done, so the reward should persist too.

Convert your past results into a “claims library.” For each project, record baseline metrics, intervention, and outcome. This becomes the proof that justifies the equity ask.

Case Study: The Contractor Turned Partner

In 2018, a Los Angeles renovation firm named Buildwell Group began offering a new proposal to investors.

Instead of charging their full project management markup of 20%, they would take half that number plus a 10% ownership stake in the finished property.

They called it sweat equity alignment.

Over five years, Buildwell accumulated minority positions in more than 20 projects.

When one of those apartment buildings sold, its equity payout exceeded the total fees they had earned across all other jobs that year.

They stopped being contractors. They became Collaborators. The lesson is universal. You do not need to own the project to own part of the upside.

You will see the same leverage in parallel lanes. Boutique architects take a small share of developer profits when their design elevates absorption and price. Short-term rental operators who begin as service providers negotiate profit shares once their systems prove a lift in NOI.

Performance marketers who control a steady inbound pipeline convert retainers into revenue partnerships or placement deals inside larger investor networks. Debt strategists who structure seller financing or assemble capital stacks take a small back end to make the transaction viable. Different crafts, one rule, expertise is capital.

Positioning, From Vendor to Partner

Equity asks feel natural when proof is visible. Publish short case notes that show baseline, intervention, and outcome; add two client quotes and one number that changed. When the lift is undeniable, propose a pilot with vesting on milestones, narrow scope of control, and a simple reporting cadence. Confidence plus clarity lowers risk for the owner and raises acceptance for you.

Forms of Collaborative Equity

There are five common structures.

Performance-based profit shares.

A professional contributes work or expertise in exchange for a percentage of profits above a baseline. For example, a property manager might receive fifteen percent of net profits after operating costs.

Equity for service exchanges.

Partners receive partial ownership in place of cash. This is common among marketing, design, or legal teams that join early-stage developments.

Deferred compensation with conversion rights.

Service providers accept reduced pay now with the option to convert unpaid fees into equity once financing stabilizes.

Joint venture participation

Specialists contribute specific deliverables such as zoning approval, construction, or branding in return for proportional stakes in the joint venture entity.

Licensing or royalty agreements.

When intellectual property such as branding, technology, or design systems drives revenue, the creator earns ongoing royalties that are linked to performance.

Each structure aligns effort with outcome and transforms service providers into silent partners.

Choose the instrument that matches the lever. If your contribution repeats across many clients, royalties or licensing often outperforms. If your value is concentrated in one asset, profit share or a small membership interest aligns better. The right shape keeps incentives clean and arguments rare.

The Psychology of Partnership

Collaborators think like investors, not employees. They view every engagement through three questions.

- Can I make this client make more money?
- Can I prove it with data?
- Can I tie my reward to that improvement?

If the answer is yes, they propose a partnership rather than payment. It is not about ego. It is about alignment. Owners respect confidence that is backed by results. They want partners who take risks and share rewards.

Disarm fear with clarity. Partners worry about permanence, control, and measurement. Offer vesting based on milestones, a narrow scope of control, and a reporting cadence everyone can see.

Case Study: The Designer Who Owned the Brand

Interior designer Mara Levin specialized in boutique hospitality. After years of billing hourly, she realized her work directly drove higher revenue through better guest experience and socially friendly interiors.

In 2021, she proposed a new approach to a developer client. She would receive a three percent profit share on net operating income for any property where she provided full branding and design.

Within two years, her company held profit shares in five boutique hotels. Her passive income exceeded her active income. Her creative vision became an annuity. This is the Collaborator mindset in action.

Build once, earn forever.

Protect your upside with a tail. If the property sells or management changes, profit share continues for a defined period or converts to a fixed payout. Your work should not vanish when ownership rotates.

Why It Works: The Law of Perceived Value

Owners chase outcomes, not invoices. If you can quantify how your expertise improves income, reduces cost, or accelerates timelines, you have leverage.

Collaborators sell certainty, not labor. They frame their contribution as an investment multiplier. For example,

- My redesign will raise average nightly rates by 18%, or,
- My marketing funnel will generate 2000 qualified buyers per month, or,
- My financing structure will reduce debt service by $7,000 per month.

When results are measurable, the partnership feels natural.

Offer a pilot. Prove lift in ninety days with a right to convert fees into equity at a preset valuation. Risk declines, trust rises.

Examples across the Industry

Here are several roles and how collaboration changes their reward.

Profession	**Usual Role**	**Collaborative Model**	**Result**
Contractor	Paid per job	Takes % of project equity	Shares in appreciation
Stager / Designer	Paid per home	Receives a bonus tied to the sale price	Alignment with seller success
Lender	Charges the origination fee	Takes backend profit share	Recurring income

Profession	Usual Role	Collaborative Model	Result
Broker / Agent	Commission only	JV partner in development	Ownership upside
Property Manager	Fixed fee	Profit-share on NOI growth	Motivated management
Marketer	Monthly retainer	Revenue-share based on lead conversions	Scalable cash flow

Across each category, the pivot from service to stake unlocks exponential results.

Framework: The Three Cs of Collaboration

There are three steps to every durable collaboration.

- **Contribution** – which is the measurable value you bring, whether time, systems, or relationships.
- **Conversion** – which is how that value converts into equity or profit share.
- **Continuity** – which is the ongoing involvement that protects and grows your stake.

Without all three, collaboration collapses into another gig. With them, you become indispensable.

Structuring the Deal

Collaborative deals need clarity, not complexity. Here's how to protect both sides.

Define deliverables and duration.

Spell out exactly what you will do, by when, and what constitutes completion.

Establish valuation.

For example, in exchange for $50,000 worth of services, Partner receives 5% equity.

Decide the equity type.

- Profit equity is a share of profits only.
- Ownership equity is the actual membership interest in the entity.

Outline payout timing.

Whether quarterly, annually, or upon sale or refinance.

Buy-out or vesting clause.

This protects both parties if the partnership ends early.

Consult legal counsel

Always execute through a formal operating agreement or a convertible contract.

Simple and transparent terms build trust and longevity.

Negotiation Snippets You Can Reuse

Pilot to profit, "We will run a 90 pilot at a reduced fee. If we exceed the targets we agree on today, you convert the difference into a small profit share for the next nine months."

Equity for service, "We can discount twenty percent of fees in exchange for a three percent profit interest that vests on delivery and goes on a tail if ownership changes."

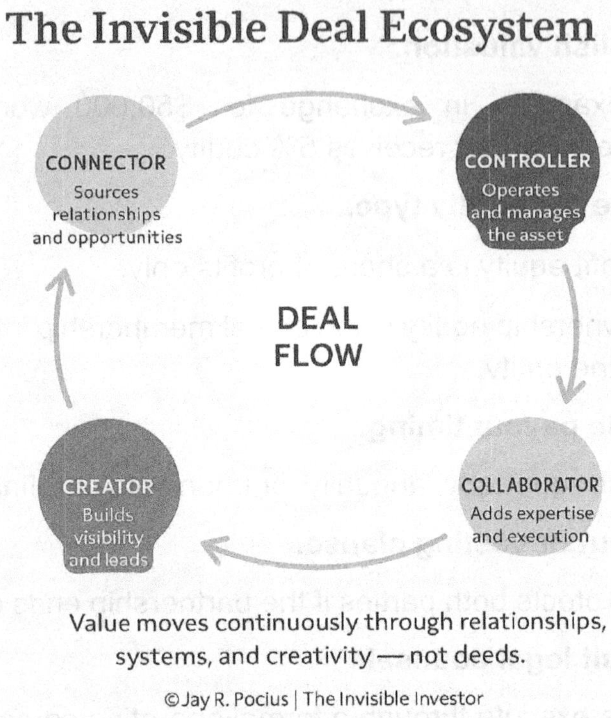

Back-end clarity, "Distributions are quarterly, tied to your P and L, with read-only dashboard access so we see the same numbers."

Mini Framework Calculating Collaborative Equity

Here is a quick rule of thumb. If your contribution improves revenue or reduces cost by a certain percent, you can often justify 1/10th to 1/5th of that improvement as ongoing participation.

For example, your marketing strategy increases monthly revenue by $10,000. A 10% share of that upside equals $1,000 per month in ongoing income.

Over a year, that is $12,000 of passive revenue, which is similar to a 12% yield on intellectual effort. You created a recurring income stream from a single project.

Case Study: Property Manager to Partner

A Florida management company called Seaside Operations managed 150 vacation homes. Instead of charging a 20% management fee, the company began offering a 10% fee plus a 10% profit share for select owners.

Some owners were skeptical at first. Then they saw results. Revenue per home jumped 30% within six months due to dynamic pricing and a direct booking strategy.

Owners earned more net income. Seaside earned recurring back-end profit. The firm became so profitable that it stopped onboarding standard management clients. Its partners now describe it as "the management company that owns nothing but earns a share of everything."

Skill as Currency

In invisible investing, skill is currency. Unlike dollars, skill appreciates with use. Every deal you collaborate on adds credibility, references, and leverage for the next one.

A top marketer who helped sell ten developments is not simply an expert. They are a rainmaker. Their portfolio of results becomes a track record that investors will gladly share equity with. The true wealth of the Collaborator lies in compounding credibility.

Technology and Collaboration

Modern tools make collaboration seamless.

- Smart contracts can automate revenue share payouts.
- Project management platforms such as Asana and Notion keep every stakeholder aligned.
- Digital signatures and secure escrow tools (HelloSign, Escrow.com) make remote agreements simple.

The Collaborator advantage is to be visible, verifiable, and scalable. One systemized partnership model can replicate across dozens of clients worldwide.

A good approach is to automate the measurement. Connect booking or sales systems to a shared dashboard so both sides see the same truth. Disputes shrink when data is visible.

Legal and Tax Considerations

There are four points to keep in view.

LLC membership versus profit interest.

Ownership equity involves capital accounts and potential liability. Profit interest grants a share of profits without initial capital and is often safer for service providers.

Taxation.

Profit interests are often taxed as capital gains when realized, not as ordinary income, but always consult a licensed tax professional.

Documentation.

Formalize every deal. Handshake agreements dissolve trust.

Liability protection.

Maintain your own entity when entering joint ventures. A well-structured agreement turns creative collaboration into a legitimate investment.

The Collaborator Mindset

Collaborators think like investors who carry a toolbox. They do not chase gigs. They chase alignment. They focus on deals where their skill can multiply value, not where it is merely used.

They know that reputation compounds faster than capital, and that the best opportunities come to the person who makes every project more profitable. That positioning attracts deals naturally.

Say no to low-leverage tasks. Protect calendar space for the few projects where your contribution is a needle mover.

Case Study: The Marketing Partnership

In 2022, a digital marketing agency called LeadFlow Partners approached a regional homebuilder with a simple pitch. We will handle your entire digital lead generation and automation at no cost for 90 days.

If it produces more than 300 qualified buyer inquiries per month, we receive 5% of every home sold for the next year. The builder agreed.

By month four, sales volume increased by 40%. LeadFlow now earns more from the profit share than it would have from all prior retainers combined.

The firm does not own land. It owns the pipeline.

Framework: The Collaboration Ladder

- **Vendor**: Paid once for work performed.
- **Preferred Partner**: Retained for recurring services.
- **Profit Collaborator**: Shares revenue upside.
- **Equity Partner**: Owns part of the project or brand.
- **Strategic Co-Founder**: Helps originate and structure deals from the start.

Each rung increases both reward and responsibility, and resilience. When markets shift, the Collaborator still earns. When projects sell, they share the win.

Climb the ladder by design. Start with a paid diagnostic, convert to a retainer, add a pilot profit share, then negotiate equity on renewal after proof.

The Compound Effect of Collaboration

Every partnership plants a seed. Five small equity positions across successful projects can create the equivalent of an entire property portfolio without any financing.

For example, a 5% profit share in five projects that average $1M in profit equals $250,000 in total share. There is no capital invested. There is only expertise that has been leveraged.

Ethical Collaboration

Partnerships only thrive when transparency rules. Collaborators should disclose conflicts, track contributions, and ensure that all parties understand expectations.

Integrity builds repeat business. Exploitation destroys ecosystems. The ultimate advantage is trust. Guard it carefully.

A perfect way to do this is by publishing a one-page ethics statement. Promise clear disclosures, measured outcomes, and choice for consumers. It signals the kind of partner you are.

Why Collaboration Wins

There are five reasons.

- **Low Capital Barrier** – Start with knowledge, not money.
- **Aligned Incentives** – Everyone wins together.
- **Scalable Model** – Same expertise, multiple deals.

- **Network Effect** – Each success attracts the next opportunity.
- **Resilience** – Income diversified across projects.

The Collaborator thrives in every cycle because expertise does not depreciate.

Fieldwork: Identify one current client where your work clearly moves revenue. Propose a 90-day pilot to trade ten percent of fees for a small profit share with a conversion option. Make the next step easy to say yes to.

The Collaborator path pairs cleanly with the other three archetypes. A Creator with distribution can attach advisory equity to growth projects. A Controller with a proven playbook can take small stakes for NOI lift. A Connector with rare access can hold a thin advisory slice in exchange for introductions that close. Collaboration is the stitching that turns roles into a portfolio.

Conclusion: The Wealth of Partnership

The Collaborator represents the evolution of professional value in the real estate economy.

They blur the line between service provider and stakeholder. They prove that ownership is not about title. It is about participation.

When you exchange knowledge for equity rather than a check, you stop working for money and start working with money.

That is the quiet revolution of invisible investing. In this new economy, the most valuable asset is not property; it is a partnership.

Next, in Chapter Seven, The Control Model in Action, we connect all four archetypes into a single operational system and show how Connectors, Controllers, Creators, and Collaborators form integrated and scalable ecosystems that generate recurring wealth without holding title.

The Control Model in Action

Personal effort hits a ceiling, systems do not. The invisible investor scales by turning conversations into pipelines, fixes into playbooks, and decisions into defaults. When outcomes arrive from mechanisms rather than willpower, the business compounds while you think. That is the quiet advantage of control.

The Invisible Investor Ecosystem

By now, the framework is clear.

- The Connector controls relationships.
- The Controller controls operations.
- The Creator controls attention.
- The Collaborator controls value exchange.

Individually, each model can produce income. Together, they form an ecosystem that compounds leverage and reduces risk.

The "Control Model" is not only about mastering assets that you do not own.

It is about orchestrating people, systems, and data in ways that produce continuous value without the friction of ownership. It is wealth creation through coordination.

Treat the four roles like departments inside one operating system. Connection, Operations, Media, and Expertise.

Each has a lead, a scorecard, and a weekly cadence. When cadence is kept, the flywheel spins.

From Chaos to System

Traditional investors build portfolios. Invisible investors build systems.

A portfolio collects things. A system connects them.

That connection between data, people, and process is where compounding begins.

You do not need a hundred doors to earn like an investor. You need a control loop that generates, monetizes, and reinvests opportunity.

Document your loop on one page: source of leads, conversion step, delivery engine, improvement cycle.

Set time targets for each handoff. The less time between steps, the more money the system prints.

From Chaos to Order, Why Most Operators Never Compound

The common trap is reactive work that consumes attention without creating assets. A simple test exposes it; if you cannot hand a process to someone else with a one-page checklist and a target metric, it is not a system, it is you. Build the checklist, set the metric, then step back and watch accuracy improve.

The Control Equation

Here is a simple way to remember the idea.

Control + Systems = Compounding Leverage

Where:

- Control means influence over how value moves, not necessarily ownership.
- Systems are repeatable processes that operate without constant input.
- Leverage means doing more with less and scaling outcomes faster than resources.

Combine these forces, and you create an **Invisible Asset Engine**.

What Is an Invisible Asset Engine?

An Invisible Asset Engine is a set of connected systems that do three things.

- Generate opportunities such as leads, deals, and partnerships.
- Monetize those inputs through service, control, or collaboration.
- Reinvest output, such as data, reputation, and profits, to fuel future growth.

In other words, it is an automated ecosystem that turns control into cash flow.

Every modern empire, from Airbnb to Blackstone to Keller Williams, operates a version of this model. They may use different terms, but the architecture is the same.

Control inputs → automate processes → compound outputs.

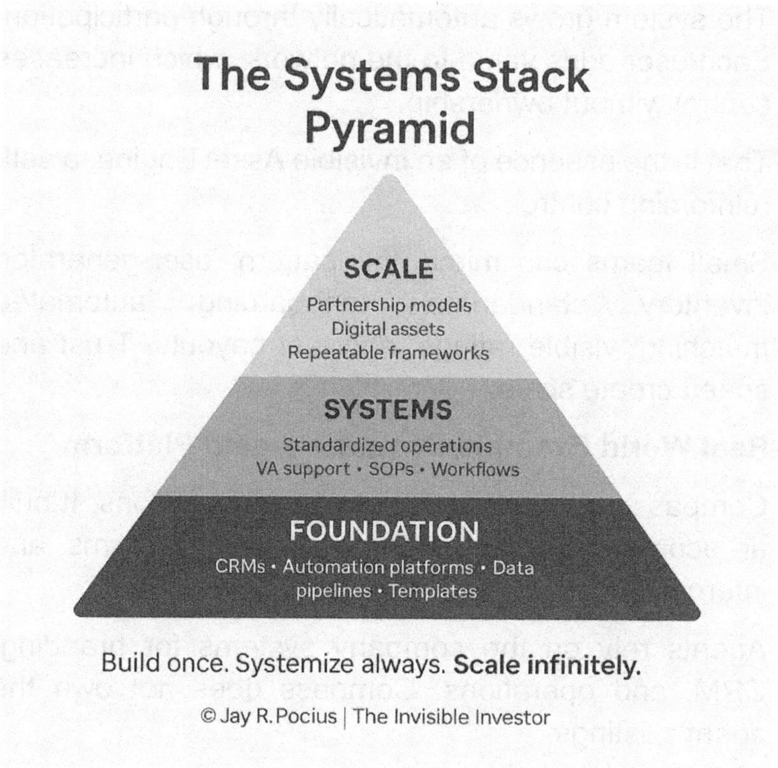

Real World Example: Airbnb Control Loop

Airbnb does not own properties, but it has built a multibillion-dollar control model.

- Input: Hosts list homes (user-generated inventory).
- Process: Airbnb manages discovery, bookings, and payments.
- Output: Guests book; hosts earn; Airbnb collects fees.
- Feedback: Reviews add credibility and improve search ranking, which drives more bookings.

The system grows automatically through participation. Each user adds value to the network, which increases control without ownership.

That is the essence of an Invisible Asset Engine, a self-reinforcing control.

Small teams can mimic the pattern: user-generated inventory, standardized onboarding, automated matching, visible ratings, and fast payouts. Trust and speed create scale.

Real World Example Compass Agent Platform

Compass does not rely solely on commissions. It built an ecosystem of tech tools, marketing platforms, and internal lending to control workflow.

Agents rely on the company systems for branding, CRM, and operations. Compass does not own the agent's listings.

It controls the infrastructure they depend on. This creates stickiness, which is recurring revenue through dependence rather than property.

It is invisible leverage that looks like support.

Your version can be a shared CRM, a library of ready-to-use campaigns, and central vendor contracts that lower costs for every partner. Shared infrastructure creates gravity.

The Invisible Machinery behind Each Archetype

Connector, a CRM that remembers every promise and routes intros with automated follow-ups.

Controller, a pricing rule set, a task engine, vendor SLAs, and a weekly scorecard that removes drift.

Creator, a publishing cadence, a hub and spoke SEO map, analytics that tie pages to revenue, not page views.

Collaborator, playbooks, templates, and a shared dashboard that make outcomes repeatable across clients.

What looks like talent from outside is usually machinery inside.

The Framework of Integration

To operate invisible investing, align the four archetypes into one coherent flow.

Generate Opportunity (The Creator + Connector)

- The Creator builds digital visibility through websites, search funnels, and social content.
- The Connector builds relationships and referral channels that feed those funnels. Together, they control attention and access.

For example, a digital platform ranks for "Ventura County real estate investment deals" and collects inquiries from investors nationwide. Those leads are referred to local agents or managers for a fee, which is pure Connector income powered by Creator systems.

Operate the Opportunity (The Controller)

Once a deal or property emerges, the Controller structures master leases, management contracts, or partnerships that convert opportunities into cash flow.

For example, a lead from the platform becomes a short-term rental client. An operator leases and manages the property, pays the owner a fixed amount, and keeps the margin. The system turns marketing leads into managed assets without buying anything.

Multiply Value (The Collaborator)

Specialists step in to deepen profitability. Designers, contractors, and marketers exchange expertise for a percentage of improved results. For example, a designer refits the rental unit, increasing occupancy by 20%. Instead of being paid once, she earns a 10% profit share.

Automate and scale (Control Model)

Once the first loop works, the goal is full automation. Tools replace manual labor. Standardized agreements replace one-off deals. Brand and data replace individual negotiation. Now the system runs itself. You have built a machine that converts information into income.

The Four-Layer System Map

Layer	**Role**	**Function**	**Key Metric**
Attention Layer	Creator	Capture leads, build brand	Traffic, engagement
Conversion Layer	Connector	Turn leads into relationships	Referrals, deals sourced

Layer	Role	Function	Key Metric
Operation Layer	Controller	Manage and monetize assets	Occupancy, NOI, margins
Optimization Layer	Collaborator	Enhance performance	ROI lift, partner satisfaction

Each layer feeds the next. When connected, they create compounding velocity.

Building Your Invisible Ecosystem

Here's a step-by-step guide on building your own Invisible Asset Engine.

Pick your core strength.

Start with the archetype that matches your skill. Are you a marketer, an operator, a negotiator, or a technician? That is your entry point.

Add a complementary function.

Once you master one role, integrate another. A Creator should add Connector systems, such as email outreach and affiliate partners.

A Controller should add Collaborator relationships, such as designers and service pros. Each connection adds leverage.

Build your digital infrastructure.

You need three tools.

- A CRM to manage relationships, such as HubSpot or GoHighLevel.
- An automation layer for schedules, follow-ups, and reporting, such as Zapier or Make.com.
- And analytics to track metrics and decision data through tools like Data Studio or a Notion dashboard.

These form the backbone of your invisible empire.

The goal is process output, not personal output. Begin measuring days by what your systems produced, not by what you touched. When the follow-ups sent, the rates update, the content ships, and the dashboard closes the loop without you, compounding has started.

Create recurring value.

Design offers or contracts that generate monthly revenue, such as subscriptions, retainers, or management fees. Predictability is the foundation of scale.

Systemize and license.

Once your model works in one market, codify it. Turn your system into a playbook or software that you can sell or license. That is when control becomes exponential.

Case Study: The Multifamily Operator Turned Platform

A company called StayModern began by leasing ten apartments in Austin and operating them as furnished rentals. Within two years, the team realized their real advantage was not the apartments.

It was their pricing software, marketing engine, and cleaning network. They pivoted and built a software dashboard and a licensing program. They now offer their technology and vendor network to other operators for a monthly fee.

Today, StayModern earns recurring revenue from dozens of partners while holding zero leases. Their invisible asset is not property. It is the process.

Lesson: When your process outperforms your inventory, sell the process. Platforms scale faster than properties.

Why Systems Create Compounding Leverage

Twenty messages sent every day is 7,300 per year with no extra thought. One evergreen page that ranks earns leads every week without meetings. A revenue rule that adjusts price on lead-time and weekday lifts margin while you sleep. Appreciation used to be the compounding engine in real estate, now repeatable systems create a faster, controllable version of the same effect.

Automation in Practice

Invisible investors thrive on automation because control scales through consistency. Common automations include

- Lead routing (Creator → Connector CRM → Operator inbox).

- Contract e-sign workflows (Controller → Collaborator).
- Revenue tracking and payouts (Stripe, QuickBooks, or AirTable dashboards).
- Dynamic pricing or AI forecasting (PriceLabs, BeyondPricing).

Each automation replaces hours of work, reduces errors, and increases control. If ownership is assets working for you, automation is systems working for you.

Start with the ugliest manual task that repeats daily. Automate that first. The morale gain alone is worth it.

The Data Advantage

In the invisible economy, data is equity.

Every lead captured, review collected, and vendor integrated ads to your control footprint. Over time, your data becomes a proprietary moat.

Just as physical investors build land portfolios, you can build information portfolios. Firms like CoStar, AirDNA, and Zillow turned this idea into multibillion-dollar valuations by aggregating and monetizing market intelligence.

Even small operators can do the same in miniature.

- Track lead conversion rates across marketing campaigns.
- Analyze occupancy data for pricing optimization.
- Maintain CRM records that predict lifetime customer value.

Data turns invisible work into measurable wealth.

Case Study: The Local Ecosystem

In Ventura, California, a small team runs a control-based ecosystem across three verticals.

- A local real estate media site under the Creator model generates organic leads through search optimization.
- A property management division under the Controller model converts leads into managed rentals.
- A vendor marketplace under the Collaborator model partners with stagers, photographers, and lenders for recurring sponsorships.

Each part feeds the other. One lead can generate three revenue streams. The team has effectively built a local version of Zillow + Vacasa + Angi's List without owning a single property.

That is the Control Model in microcosm, connected, cash flowing, and invisible.

Protect the loop with service level agreements between internal teams. If the media site promises a lead response in one hour, the operations team must be staffed to meet it.

Internal trust powers external growth.

Scaling Through Licensing

Once a system produces consistent results, the next step is replication without ownership through licensing your playbook.

Licensing converts operational know-how into intellectual property income. You can license

- Brand templates
- Software dashboards and
- Standard operating procedures.

For example, a boutique property management firm builds a process manual and a software kit for luxury short-term rentals.

They license it to ten operators across different cities for $1,000 per month each. The result is $120,000 per year from an asset that requires no physical expansion. Licensing is ownership of influence.

The Invisible Franchise

The most advanced form of the Control Model is the invisible franchise, a brand system that unites independent operators under shared standards and technology.

Consider how Keller Williams, EXP Realty, or Real Broker operate.

They do not own the offices or the agents. They own the platform, the brand, and the system. They scale without heavy overhead because control replaces real estate.

Your invisible empire can do the same. Whether you manage short-term rentals, run local marketing portals, or coordinate renovation partners, you can create consistency without physical expansion.

- Minimum Viable Stack, A Quick Build Relationships, a simple CRM with two views, pipeline and people due today.
- Flow, one automation tool to move forms, emails, and tasks, keep the triggers few and reliable.
- Proof, a living metrics page that anyone can open without logging into five apps.
- Cadence, one weekly review with the same five numbers, trend arrows, and a single owner per fix.

Key Metrics of a Control-Based Business

Category	**Metric**	**Target**
Lead Flow	# of new opportunities per month	50+
Conversion Rate	% of leads converted	10–20%
Recurring Revenue	Monthly recurring cash flow	60–80% of income
Automation Ratio	% of tasks automated	>70%
Partner Retention	Average duration of collaboration	12+ months
Profit Margin	After expenses	30–40%

When you manage these numbers, your business begins to behave like a fund that generates predictable and compounding returns.

Mindset Shift from Doer to Designer

The hardest transition for many entrepreneurs is to move from doing to designing. Invisible investors do not run every system. They architect systems that run themselves.

Every process you design and delegate increases your control equity. It is the same concept that drives franchising, software as a service, and licensing.

Own the infrastructure, not the output. The more you automate, the more your influence compounds. That is how invisible investors retire early. They build control systems that pay them for a very long time.

The Ethical Layer

Control without ownership requires trust. Because you operate other people's assets, brands, or data, ethical alignment matters more than legal authority. Transparency is non-negotiable.

- Always disclose revenue splits clearly.
- Do not withhold performance data.
- Prioritize long-term relationships over short-term profit.

Your reputation is your equity. Lose that and your control dissolves quickly.

The Flywheel Effect

The Control Model aims to build a flywheel, a self-sustaining cycle of opportunity, income, and reinvestment.

The flywheel flow.

- Visibility (Creator) generates leads.
- Access (Connector) turns them into relationships.
- Execution (Controller) produces income.
- Improvement (Collaborator) boosts results.
- Reputation attracts more visibility.

Round and round it goes, faster each cycle. That is compounding control.

That is invisible wealth.

Case Study: The Mini Empire Model

A small team of four professionals can control millions in revenue through integrated systems.

- A marketing specialist acts as the Creator.
- A networker or deal source acts as the Connector.
- An operator acts as the Controller.
- A designer or contractor acts as the Collaborator.

Together, they manage a portfolio of leased, managed, and co-branded properties, none owned outright. Their collective strength is coordination. This is how boutique empires form, quietly, efficiently, and profitably.

Systems create financial leverage and psychological leverage. Decision fatigue drops, fire drills fade, and calendar space reappears for design and strategy. That calm is not a luxury, it is part of the return, because clear thinking raises conversion and lowers churn.

Conclusion: The Architecture of Freedom

Control is the new currency of wealth. It rewards creativity, execution, and collaboration rather than capital. The Control Model turns the chaos of modern real estate into a cohesive, automated machine.

It allows small teams to outperform larger investors and lets creators scale without debt. Ownership was yesterday's security. Control is tomorrow's freedom.

In the next chapter, we will explore how to monetize access itself, the highest layer of invisible investing, where community, data, and credibility become the new asset class.

Action prompt: Write your one-page operating system today. Name the four leads, list five core metrics, set the weekly meetings, and pick one bottleneck to remove in the next fourteen days.

Monetizing Access

If control is the engine of invisible wealth, then access is the fuel that allows the engine to run at full capacity. Access has become one of the most powerful revenue drivers in the modern economy, not access to property, but access to people, information, networks, insights, and opportunity flow. In the traditional real estate world, value was held in physical assets. In the invisible economy, value is held in the channels that connect people to those assets. Whoever controls the channels controls the outcomes.

Access is the invisible investor's version of ownership, a form of leverage that is softer, more adaptable, and far more scalable than holding physical property. Access does not depend on capital reserves, loan approvals, renovation budgets, or maintenance costs. It depends on your position within a network and your ability to curate information that others find valuable. And because access is intangible, it can grow exponentially. A person can only own so many buildings, but they can build influence with unlimited reach.

For decades, access was always valuable, but it was difficult to monetize. People acted as informal connectors within their communities, introducing investors to agents, contractors to developers, buyers to lenders. These introductions created plenty of value, yet few people knew how to structure compensation around their contributions. Today, the world has shifted. Technology has made it easier to track introductions, measure engagement, formalize communities, and build platforms where access itself becomes a structured financial asset.

Communities, audiences, and networks have become the digital equivalent of land. They are spaces people gather, spaces people trust, spaces people rely on to navigate complex markets. And because these spaces are scarce, those who build them command extraordinary leverage.

The most successful real estate operators today often have little interest in being the loudest or most visible figure in the room. But they are intentional about cultivating environments where people come to them. They might build an online community where investors share deals. They might produce a local newsletter that residents read religiously. They might create a monthly meetup that becomes the place where introductions happen. They might teach classes, speak at events, join panels, or publish guides that position them as a knowledgeable authority. All of these activities create pathways for people to enter their orbit. Once people consistently enter your orbit, monetization emerges naturally.

The power of access lies in the trust that forms around it. When someone consistently shows up with valuable insights, thoughtful curation, or reliable information, they become someone people look to for guidance.

And in a world as complex and emotionally charged as real estate, guidance is invaluable. Buyers feel uncertain. Sellers feel cautious. Investors feel overwhelmed. Operators feel stretched thin. Access to clarity becomes access to opportunity.

This is why access monetization has quietly become one of the most profitable models in the industry. People will pay for communities that help them grow. They will pay for coaching that sharpens their strategy. They will pay for newsletters that save them time. They will pay for introductions that accelerate their goals. They will pay for guidance that reduces risk. And they will pay for tools that improve their decision-making.

The invisible investor recognizes that attention is not enough. Attention is fleeting; access is enduring. Attention creates moments; access creates momentum. A person can go viral and still fail to monetize. A person with access, however, can create recurring revenue without needing mass visibility.

The New Currency of Real Estate

In the traditional model, wealth flowed to whoever owned property. Today, it flows to whoever owns access.

Access is the bridge between capital, opportunity, and execution. It is the invisible infrastructure that connects people who have deals with the people who can make those deals work.

Access is not luck, popularity, or charisma. It is distribution power. Who you can reach, what you can influence, and how quickly you can move information are now more valuable than ownership itself.

The modern real estate economy rewards those who create connections on a scale and who know how to structure those connections for profit.

The shift is practical, not philosophical. Owners face heavy capital requirements and slow cycles. Access builders launch faster, test faster, and compound faster because the product is relationship flow. The investor who controls the on-ramp to deals often earns senior economics without touching the deed.

Access as an Asset Class

In a world shaped by networks, access behaves like equity. Consider the parallels.

- A property gives you rental income.
- A network gives you deal flow.
- A database gives you leverage.
- A brand gives you trust.

Together, these are assets that produce ongoing yield without the burden of ownership.

Access compounds. Every introduction, referral, and shared collaboration strengthens the infrastructure that surrounds your business. The stronger your access, the less capital you need.

That is why senior investors and entrepreneurs spend more time building relationships than buying properties.

Case Study: BiggerPockets and the Power of Community

BiggerPockets shows what monetized access looks like in real life. It began as an online forum for investors and evolved into a content and community platform with millions of members.

BiggerPockets does not sell properties. It sells connection. The business earns through memberships, sponsorships, events, and advertising.

All of it is fueled by trust and engagement. The core product is access to people who share your goals. A Pro membership includes data and calculators.

What members truly pay for is proximity to knowledge, deals, mentors, and momentum.

That is the hidden yield of access.

The engine works because the community is curated and productive. Questions are answered, deals are vetted, and track records become visible. When the signal stays high, members happily fund the platform that protects it.

The Access Economy

The shift from ownership to access is visible across the modern economy.

- Uber gives you transportation without owning cars.
- Airbnb gives you places to stay without owning property.
- WeWork gives you offices without owning buildings.

- MasterClass gives you mentorship without personal contact.

Real estate follows the same logic. You no longer need to own the asset if you can monetize access to people who do.

Access has become the universal language of leverage.

In practice, access wins when it removes friction. If your platform reduces the search cost for the right lender, the right operator, or the right JV partner, the market will pay you every month to keep the gates open and orderly.

Types of Access You Can Monetize

Access to information

- Market data, insider knowledge, and deal flow.
- Examples include paid newsletters and data dashboards.

Access to people

- Private networks, masterminds, communities, and introductions.
- Examples include curated investor circles and private communication groups.

Access to education

- Online courses, workshops, and mentorship programs

- Examples include investor boot camps, training series, and coaching programs

Access to opportunity

- Exclusive listings, partnerships, and off-market deals
- Example deal clubs, fund introductions, and syndication communities

Each category can produce recurring and scalable revenue. You do not need to own property. You need proximity to people who do.

Design each access product with a clear promise. Tell members exactly what outcomes to expect each month. Examples include five vetted introductions, two exclusive deal briefs, or one closed-door session with an operator who shares numbers. Specific promises create retention.

Case Study: Keller Williams and the Wealth Network

Keller Williams is the largest real estate franchise in the world. Its greatest product is not brokerage. Its greatest product is access.

Through systems such as KW Connect and Command, agents gain access to shared databases of listings and buyers, to training resources, internal referral networks, and cultural alignment through masterminds and events.

KW earns through franchise royalties and technology licensing. The entire engine runs on internal access.

Thousands of independent agents operate like one interconnected organism. That is monetized access on a global scale.

Notice the structure. The company converts individual effort into network effects through common tools and shared language. That is access institutionalized.

Framework: The Access Pyramid

Level	Type	Example	Monetization
Tier 1	Open Access	Free content, public community	Ad revenue, sponsorships
Tier 2	Guided Access	Paid courses, mentorship	Subscriptions, one-time sales
Tier 3	Curated Access	Private groups, masterminds	Membership fees
Tier 4	Exclusive Access	Deal partnerships, co-investing	Equity shares, performance fees

Your goal as an Invisible Investor is to build all four levels so you gain both reach and exclusivity. The top tiers require trust and produce the highest margins.

Move members upward by delivering increasing specificity. Start with broad education, graduate them into focused rooms, then invite the top performers into co-investment. Each step narrows the room while raising the value.

Case Study: Tony Robbins and Strategic Influence

Tony Robbins does not sell real estate, yet he embodies the monetization of access. Through private events and investment partnerships, he turns relationships into recurring income.

Live events act as ecosystems of deal flow. High net worth attendees meet fund managers, developers, and service providers, and partnerships often form on the spot.

The business earns from

- event tickets
- sponsorships
- coaching memberships
- and investment participation rights.

He earns not only by selling access but by owning the system that grants it.

That is the Access Engine in action.

The portable lesson is to own the container. When the room, the agenda, and the follow-up all sit inside your brand, value created inside that container is naturally routed back to you.

The Access Engine

Network + Platform + Monetization = Access Engine

An Access Engine turns your network into a product. It connects people through a platform and charges for participation, visibility, or opportunity.

Every major modern brand runs some version of this engine.

- LinkedIn monetizes connections.
- Facebook monetizes attention.
- Zillow monetizes buyer and seller access.
- Real estate coaches monetize mentorship access.

In each case, the infrastructure is the asset.

Build your engine to reduce work for both sides. Standardized profiles, verified credentials, and template introductions shorten the path from first contact to signed term sheet. Engines that save time always gain market share.

How to Build an Access Engine

1. Identify your niche

Choose the audience you will serve. Investors, agents, lenders, vendors, or homeowners. You cannot be the gatekeeper for everyone. Specialize.

2. Build a platform

Start small. Create a communication group, a simple website with gated resources, or a recurring meetup or online mastermind. Deliver value and connection first. Monetization follows engagement.

3. Curate relationships

Do not chase volume. Curate quality. A small and trusted group beats a large and passive following.

4. Layer in monetization

Once the value is proven, add paid tiers.

- Premium subscriptions for insider access.
- Sponsorships for brands seeking visibility.
- Event fees for live networking.

Each layer adds recurring revenue.

Automate and scale

Automate onboarding, billing, and communications. As your access grows, maintain exclusivity. Scarcity increases perceived value.

Ninety-day Launch Plan

Days 1 to 7

Define avatar and promises, days 8 to 21, publish a free resource, and host one open call.

Days 22 to 45

Pre-sell founding memberships with a cap of fifty, days 46 to 60 onboard sponsors with a one-page media kit.

Days 61 to 90

Deliver two flagship sessions and a private directory. Measure join rate, attendance, and referral invites.

Case Study: The Boutique Investor Network

A small California team created a private group for accredited investors who focus on short-term rentals. Membership included access to vetted operators, lenders, and markets. For $99 per month, members received

- Monthly deal packets,
- Group calls with property managers, and,
- A shared channel for introductions.

Within one year, the group reached 500 members and $6,000 in annual recurring revenue. They did not sell properties. They sold access to the people who had them.

Pricing models that work

- Tiered memberships at $49 and $99 per month, with clear limits on introductions and event seats.
- Sponsors at $1000 to $5000 per month with guaranteed placements and reporting.
- Per introduction fees only where regulations allow and with written consent.

Building Access Equity

Access equity is the trust, the data, and the distribution you own over time. Every contact, every piece of shared knowledge, and every partnership adds to that equity.

It does not depreciate. Three dimensions define your access equity.

- **Reach** – How many people can you connect with?
- **Relevance** – How valuable your network is to your niche.
- **Responsiveness** – How quickly you can mobilize your network.

High access equity means you're never out of business, because opportunity always finds you first.

Data as Access

In the digital age, data is access to everything. Knowing who to reach and when to reach them is a monetize-able skill.

Platforms such as CoStar, CoreLogic, and Redfin thrive because their databases reduce friction between need and solution. Small operators can mirror the model in miniature.

- Build email lists that are segmented by buyer type.
- Maintain databases of verified service providers.
- Track lead behavior to personalize outreach.

You do not need to own the data. You need to organize it. That is where the value lives.

The Power of Community

Access monetizes best when it forms around shared identity. People join to belong first and to transact second.

The most successful access-based businesses build culture as a foundation.

- BiggerPockets built investor camaraderie.
- Compass built a community for agents.
- eXp Realty built a shared ownership culture.
- Local investor meetups build trust that outlives any contract.
- Y Combinator built an alumni-powered founder network.

Treat the community as infrastructure, supporting a scalable network.

What makes access so financially powerful is its emotional gravity. Real estate is complex, high-stakes, and often intimidating. People crave certainty, they crave context, and they crave a sense of belonging while they make big decisions. Most investors do not want to “go it alone.” They want to move with peers who understand the terrain.

When you create a space that delivers clarity, reduces isolation, and normalizes ambition, you are building more than a room; you are building an ongoing form of mentorship. Access, delivered with integrity, becomes mentorship at scale. It is leadership without hierarchy, influence without ownership, and value without the grind of traditional labor.

In that environment, fees feel less like a cost and more like a contribution. Members know the room is curated, the information filtered, and the standards guarded. That is why the right community can sustain premium pricing year after year while low-quality groups churn. The true product is not content; it is confidence.

Framework: The Access Ladder

Stage	Description	Example
Connect	Build relationships through free value (content, events).	Blog, podcast, social media
Engage	Deepen with personal interactions.	Mastermind, Q&A session
Curate	Filter and organize your network.	Private membership
Monetize	Offer structured value.	Paid tiers, sponsorships
Institutionalize	Turn it into a brand.	Community platform or SaaS

Each step increases value and defensibility. By the final stage, your network operates like a business that is predictable, automated, and appreciated in value.

Case Study: YPO the Global Network Effect

The Young Presidents Organization is a prime example of institutionalized access. Members pay significant annual fees for curated access to other leaders.

The value is not just the meetings. The value is the network. Deals, partnerships, and mentorships emerge because access has been intentionally designed and governed. Access, when structured well, becomes a perpetual asset.

Monetizing Access Ethically

Influence is powerful, and it carries responsibility. Ethical monetization means you

- Protect privacy and data
- Ensure that access is not exploitative
- Deliver value equal to or greater than the cost of entry, and
- Facilitate relationships rather than sell them

Sustainable access monetization builds reputation. Short-term exploitation destroys it.

Add legal guardrails. If you touch referrals or deal clubs, review RESPA, advertising disclosures, and basic securities rules for private offerings.

When in doubt, structure revenue as sponsorship or education, not contingent fees that require licensure. Being careful is part of being credible.

Pricing Access with Unit Economics

Price from outcomes not features. Start with the value of a closed deal or a filled role. Work backward to a monthly fee that makes partner money even at conservative conversion rates.

Keep acquisition cost below one-third of lifetime value and keep churn below five percent monthly. If those two numbers hold, the model will scale.

Failure Modes and How to Avoid Them

Most access businesses fail from dilution or drift. Dilution happens when the room gets too big or too noisy. Drift happens when the promise becomes fuzzy.

Fight both with tight admission, visible moderation, and a single sentence value promise you repeat on every page.

The invisible investor understands that wealth is not only about cash flow or equity. It is also about positioning. The person at the center of access, whether through digital platforms, curated communities, educational ecosystems, or deal networks, gains a kind of influence that compounds every year. Their name becomes shorthand for reliability. Their platform becomes synonymous with opportunity. Their network evolves into a marketplace of trust.

As that influence expands, the invitations change. You are no longer asked simply to participate in deals; you are asked to help shape them. Access becomes the foundation of partnership. Partnership becomes the engine of recurring revenue. And recurring revenue quietly matures into a portfolio of interests that would never show up on a typical property list, but absolutely show up in your bank account.

The Access Multiplier

Access multiplies every archetype.

- The Connector expands your reach.
- The Controller gains clients faster.
- The Creator amplifies visibility.
- The Collaborator finds aligned partners.

Every model accelerates when access is monetized. Access is the gravity that holds the ecosystem together.

Conclusion: Access Is the Asset

Owning buildings gives you stability. Owning access gives you velocity. Access cannot burn down, flood, or depreciate. It appreciates through use.

In the era of invisible investing, control of access to information, to opportunity, and to community is the ultimate leverage point. Those who structure it, protect it, and monetize it will outperform owners in every cycle.

Ownership can build wealth. Access builds empires.

In the next chapter, you will learn how to measure and manage your invisible portfolio so your systems, data, relationships, and influence show up on a personal balance sheet that proves your wealth even when you own nothing at all.

Building the Invisible Portfolio

Every investor understands the concept of a portfolio, a curated collection of assets that, together, represent stability, diversification, and long-term potential. For years, portfolios were synonymous with property ownership, a rental home here, a duplex there, maybe an apartment building or a handful of short-term rentals. The thinking was simple, the more doors you owned, the stronger your financial foundation.

But the invisible investor plays by a different rulebook. The portfolio they build isn't made of physical structures. It isn't composed of units, doors, or deeds. Instead, it's composed of leverage, influence, systems, partnerships, and recurring opportunities. Their portfolio lives beyond the constraints of walls and land. It grows in the digital realm, in the relational realm, and in the strategic realm, areas where returns are often faster, risks are lower, and growth is constrained only by creativity.

The invisible portfolio isn't built through capital deployment; it's built through leverage creation. It is the practical expression of the idea that wealth is not about owning assets, but about controlling outcomes.

The Myth of the Missing Portfolio

Many investors measure success by what they can touch. Doors, deeds, and deposits. Yet the assets they control and the systems they have built often produce just as much income and never appear on a balance sheet.

That is your Invisible Portfolio.

It is the set of relationships, systems, intellectual property, and influence that generate wealth without ownership.

If you have ever created a lead funnel, licensed a system, built a network, or managed assets for others, you already have an invisible portfolio.

You simply have not quantified it yet.

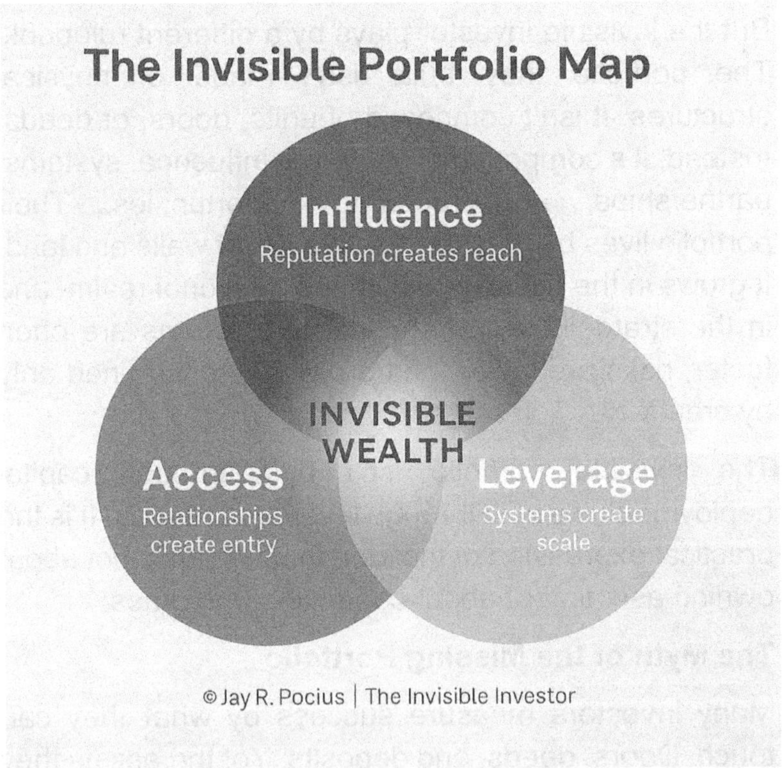

Quantification matters because it changes behavior. When you can see the value of a newsletter, a playbook, or a partner roster expressed in cash flow and multiples, you maintain it with the same rigor you would apply to a physical building.

The New Definition of a Portfolio

In the invisible economy, a portfolio is not a list of what you own; it is a reflection of what you influence. It includes the systems you operate, the platforms you build, the partnerships you maintain, the communities you nurture, the digital assets you create, and the operational engines you control.

A traditional investor might show you a binder with property records.

An invisible investor could show you:

- A digital funnel that captures investment leads every day
- A newsletter that keeps thousands of readers engaged
- A network of operators who rely on their introductions
- A partnership agreement that generates recurring revenue
- A master-leased property managed with zero ownership obligations
- A content platform that investors trust and share
- A system that analyzes deals or manages operations without manual effort

- A community where opportunities are exchanged organically

Even without lists and bullet points, the essence is simple, an invisible portfolio is not a collection of properties; it is a collection of leverage.

No deletions needed; this dovetails nicely with your "Redefining 'Asset'" section, which zooms in from portfolio to individual asset level.

Redefining "Asset"

An asset is anything that produces future economic benefit. That definition does not require title, land, or a loan. It includes

- Website that produces leads,
- Partnership that pays a profit share,
- Management agreement,
- Digital product that sells automatically and,
- Network that feeds referrals.

If it generates income or influence, it is an asset. When you can systemize it, it behaves like equity even if it remains invisible to accountants.

The Invisible Portfolio reframes wealth from what you own to what you control and can repeat.

A working test is simple. If you stopped today, would the asset still earn next month? If yes, it belongs on your invisible balance sheet.

The Portfolio without Property

Let's compare two investors.

Investor A owns three rentals that generate $1,000 per month each after expenses. Total net income is $3,000 per month.

Investor B manages 10 vacation rentals for other owners and earns $3,000 per month per property through fees and profit shares.

Total net income is also $3,000 per month.

Investor A has $1.5 million tied up in equity. Investor B has almost no capital at risk. Both earn the same cash flow.

Only one can reinvest, replicate, or pivot instantly. That is the power of an invisible portfolio. It frees capital and compounds systems.

This example is not anti-ownership. It is pro-optionality. The strongest operators often hold a few great assets while growing a much larger halo of invisible ones.

Case Study: The Digital Syndicator

RealNet Growth, a Miami marketing firm, specializes in online buyer leads for developers.

Instead of one-off lead fees, it took 1% equity participation in every project its systems helped sell out. Five years later, it held small stakes in 14 developments; most were under 1%, yet the total equity topped $2.8 million.

They did not own property. They owned participation in performance. That is invisible equity, scalable, liquid, and resilient.

The key was documentation. Deals flowed because the firm could show consistent cost per qualified lead and a clean trail from campaign to sales ledger. Proof unlocks participation.

The Architecture of an Invisible Portfolio

What makes an invisible portfolio so powerful is its interconnected nature. Each asset in the portfolio amplifies the others. A digital presence strengthens partnerships. Partnerships strengthen deal flow. Deal flow strengthens influence. Influence strengthens community. Community strengthens monetization. And monetization, in turn, feeds everything else. It behaves more like a loop than a ladder.

Instead of climbing upward one rung at a time, the invisible investor builds outward, expanding in multiple directions at once.

A Creator might begin with a single website that generates a few leads each month. Over time, that website grows into a network of online properties, each feeding a consistent flow of inbound interest. That interest sparks partnerships with lenders, agents, or operators who pay for visibility or referrals.

Those partnerships mature into profit participation in deals. Without ever purchasing a building, the Creator now owns a multi-channel income ecosystem that behaves like a diversified investment portfolio.

A Controller might start with a single master lease or operational agreement. As systems improve, they take on more properties. Their reputation compounds. Owners seek them out as the trusted operator. They negotiate better terms, gain performance-based back-end, or secure scaled management contracts. Over time, their portfolio consists of operational control spread across many assets, with none of the debt or liability associated with ownership.

The same story plays out for Connectors and Collaborators. A Connector becomes the person everyone calls for introductions. The network compounds. Influential relationships become a form of currency. That currency converts into referral fees, advisory seats, and joint ventures.

A Collaborator upgrades from service provider to strategic partner. They negotiate equity, advisory compensation, or performance-based earnings. They do not collect properties; they collect participation.

Framework: The Four Dimensions of the Invisible Portfolio

Dimension	Description	Example
Income Streams	Recurring or residual earnings.	Management fees, subscriptions, licensing.
System Equity	Owned processes, software, or brands.	CRM templates, automation, playbooks.

Dimension	Description	Example
Relationship Capital	Networks and partnerships that produce opportunities.	Referral networks, JV agreements.
Reputation Equity	Brand trust and authority that amplify reach.	Thought leadership, testimonials, social following.

Each dimension compounds differently. Income provides cash flow. Systems scale productivity. Relationships multiply deal flow.

Reputation accelerates everything. The goal is not to maximize one category. The goal is to balance all four into a resilient ecosystem.

When one dimension weakens, the others can carry the load. A quiet month in lead sales hurts less if partner retainers and course subscriptions continue to pay.

Why Invisible Portfolios Outperform

Traditional ownership offers one undeniable strength, appreciation. But appreciation is slow, cyclical, and heavily dependent on factors outside your control. It is the reward at the end of a long journey, not the daily fuel that keeps the engine moving.

An invisible portfolio, by contrast, is built to create rapid cash flow, flexibility, and adaptability. It grows through action, not acquisition. It expands through leverage, not debt. It compounds through relationships and systems, not through property prices alone. Revenue is spread across multiple streams that are not tied to the performance of a single building or a single market.

Because the assets are light and often digital, the invisible investor can step in and out of opportunities with far less friction. There is no waiting on closings, no refinancing delays, and far fewer sunk costs. The portfolio is not stuck. It is fluid.

This structure also makes the invisible portfolio naturally diversified. A traditional investor might spend years acquiring a small number of properties, each consuming capital and concentration. An invisible investor can build dozens of leverage-based assets in the same span of time, each with minimal overhead and minimal risk. The result is not just more scalability; it is more resilience.

Mapping Your Invisible Portfolio

Most investors never take inventory of what they truly own. To achieve this, you can use this exercise.

1. List every recurring income source.

Include anything that pays monthly, quarterly, or annually, such as management fees, affiliate income, software subscriptions, or digital courses.

2. List every system you have built.

Capture the processes, templates, and technologies that make you money or save you time. These assets increase efficiency and reduce dependency.

3. Map your relationships.

List your top twenty collaborators, clients, or partners.

Next to each, note:

- Frequency of engagement.
- Type of value exchanged.
- Growth potential.

4. Quantify your reputation.

Measure referral volume, audience engagement, brand mentions, and client retention. Together, these metrics define your invisible net worth.

Convert the exercise into a living dashboard. Use one page that shows income by stream, top five systems by time saved, top partners by revenue influenced, and audience growth.

Review monthly. Improvement follows visibility.

Case Study: The Boutique Ecosystem

A professional in San Diego built a mini empire with a simple formula.

- One lead-generating blog.
- One referral network of 25 agents.
- Two marketing retainers from lenders.

The ecosystem produced $15,000 per month in net income. That is the equivalent of owning $3 million in property at a 6% yield. He called it a digital duplex.

Each year, he duplicated the model in a new city. The result was a set of parallel revenue streams that required no debt and no tenants.

Within five years, the invisible portfolio produced more than $250,000 per year. He did not build houses. He built systems.

Framework: The Invisible Portfolio Matrix

Asset Type	**Tangible Example**	**Control Leverage**	**Cash Flow**	**Scale Potential**
Contractual	Management agreements, leases	Medium	High	Moderate
Digital	Websites, email lists, SaaS tools	High	Medium	High
Relational	Partnerships, referral pipelines	High	Medium	High
Intellectual	Courses, brand, automation systems	Very High	Medium	Very High

Your job as an Invisible Investor is to allocate attention and effort across all four, just as a traditional investor diversifies across asset classes.

Quantifying Invisible Equity

You can estimate portfolio value with a simple formula.

Annual Net Income × Valuation Multiple = Asset Value

Depending on the stability and scalability of your systems, the multiple often ranges from 2× to 6× annual net income, which is like how digital businesses and franchises are valued.

For example, a combined recurring income of $200,000 per year from contracts, memberships, and digital assets can support a valuation between $800,000 to $1.2 million.

When the systems are documented and transferable. That is sellable wealth even if you do not own a single property.

Case Study: CoStar the Data Portfolio

CoStar Group built a global data empire worth $30 billion by applying invisible portfolio logic. The company does not develop real estate. It owns the data about real estate.

Platforms such as Apartments.com, LoopNet, and Ten-X function as portfolio assets that produce recurring subscription income. The wealth lives in informational equity.

Each new user, each listing, and each dataset compound value. The portfolio does not rely on a single property market. It is a market of its own.

That is what invisible wealth looks like on a scale.

The Flywheel of Compounding Control

An invisible portfolio compounds faster than traditional property because it reinvests itself automatically. Every dollar earned, every relationship built, and every system improved feeds the next opportunity.

The result is a control flywheel.

The Cycle:

- Build a system (Creator).
- Monetize through relationships (Connector).
- Operate efficiently (Controller).
- Reinvest profit into partnerships (Collaborator).
- Repeat.

Each spin of the wheel increases control equity, which is your invisible net worth.

Mini Case Study: The Content Syndicate

Three marketers built niche property websites in major metros. They earn through affiliate commissions and lead sales. Then they pooled analytics into a single dashboard and licensed it to brokerages nationwide.

The combined system now earns six figures per month. The income does not come from ads or listings. It comes from access to insight.

They do not own the real estate. They own the discovery. Their portfolio is data, not dirt.

Tracking Your Portfolio

Treat your invisible assets the way a fund manager tracks holdings. You need visibility, metrics, and momentum.

Category	Metric	Target
Income Streams	Monthly recurring revenue	↑ month-over-month
Systems	Hours saved / efficiency gain	20% annual improvement
Relationships	Active partnerships	10 new per quarter
Reputation	Engagement or referrals	Consistent upward trend

Create a simple dashboard in your preferred tool (Notion, Airtable, or Google Sheets) to monitor each category. Once you measure it, you can improve it.

The Psychology of an Invisible Portfolio

There is a profound internal shift that happens when you start building an invisible portfolio. You stop thinking like an operator and start thinking like an architect. Instead of asking, "What is my next deal?" you begin asking, "What system can I build so deals find me?" You move from chasing transactions to designing recurring pathways.

You also stop measuring success purely by the number of physical assets you own. You start measuring by the amount of leverage you control, the breadth of your influence, and the depth of your systems. That mindset shift is liberating. You are no longer tethered to a building. You are tethered to a strategy. Strategies, unlike buildings, can evolve as fast as you do.

An invisible portfolio gives you permission to be more creative. It gives you access to deals you might not qualify for financially. It opens doors to rooms you would not traditionally enter. It offers scale without constant stress, growth without parallel debt, and leverage without equivalent liability.

Most importantly, it rewires confidence. When your wealth is tied to your creativity instead of your credit score, you begin to trust yourself differently. You see, in real time, that the power was never in the property lines; it was in your ability to shape outcomes.

The Liquidity Advantage

Traditional real estate is slow and illiquid. Invisible assets can be sold or transferred quickly. You can

- Sell a lead generation site on established marketplaces.
- License a management playbook to other operators.
- Transfer digital course rights.
- Sell a client list to another business.

Liquidity increases optionality. Optionality increases freedom. The invisible investor's strongest advantage is the ability to pivot.

Case Study: Exit without Entry

A marketing entrepreneur spent years creating education for agents, including blog posts, SEO courses, and templates. When it was time to move on, he sold his website and email list to a proptech company for $750,000.

No physical office. No property holdings. Only systems, subscribers, and trust. He built, scaled, and sold an invisible portfolio.

Wealth no longer requires walls.

The Invisible Portfolio Checklist

To actively grow your portfolio, review this checklist each quarter.

- **Recurring Income Audit** – How many income streams do I control that don't rely on me showing up daily?
- **System Scalability** – Which processes can I automate or license?
- **Partnership Health** – Are my relationships producing mutual value?
- **Reputation Reach** – How many people trust my brand and content?
- **Exit Readiness** – Could I sell or delegate this business tomorrow?

A full set of "yes" answers means your portfolio is both invisible and resilient.

The Hidden Compounding Effect

Each invisible asset produces its own yield and amplifies the others.

- Systems reduce costs.
- Relationships accelerate deal flow.
- Reputation enhances conversion.
- Income funds reinvestment.

The synergy across layers is exponential. That is why small invisible portfolios often outperform large physical ones. They compound along multiple dimensions at once.

Why Traditional Metrics Fail

Net worth statements measure ownership, not control. They miss the equity of influence, of reputation, and of digital infrastructure. To evaluate the invisible wealth track,

- Monthly Recurring Revenue (MRR)
- Number of Active Systems
- Network Velocity (opportunities per month) and,
- Brand Reach Metrics

Your new balance sheet looks more like a performance dashboard than a tax form.

Framework: The Invisible Portfolio Formula

Wealth = (Control × Leverage × Trust) ÷ Dependence

Where,

- Control = number of systems or relationships you influence.
- Leverage = automation and scalability of those systems.
- Trust = the strength of your brand and network.
- Dependence = how tied your income is to your personal labor.

The goal: Increase the numerator and reduce the denominator. True freedom occurs when systems and trust flourish, while dependence wanes.

Case Study: The Portfolio You Cannot See

A property technology consultant in Texas does not own a single home, yet his monthly cash flow rivals many landlords. He runs

- Three automation systems that he licenses to managers,
- Two affiliate partnerships with lenders, and,
- One professional community.

Total cash flow is $25,000 per month. Time at work is less than 30 hours per week. His portfolio is not on Zillow. It lives in an inbox, in software dashboards, and in relationships.

That is the new empire. It is borderless, low-friction, and unlimited.

Acquiring Invisible Assets

You can buy what others have built. Small newsletters, niche websites, and playbooks are often available at modest multiples when the owner wants to move on.

Do brief diligence on traffic sources, email engagement, and revenue verification. Acquire, clean, and relaunch under your systems so the asset produces more under your roof than it did under theirs.

Accounting and Tax Basics for Intangibles

Treat recurring revenue with the same discipline as rent. Separate operating income from one-time windfalls. Track acquisition costs for digital assets because they can often be amortized.

Always confirm treatment with a licensed professional. Clean books raise valuations and reduce surprises at exit.

The Freedom of Intangible Wealth

When you measure wealth by influence and systems rather than by property and possessions, your opportunities multiply. You can live anywhere, partner with anyone, and pivot quickly.

Invisible portfolios are resilient across cycles. Markets can crash, rents can drop, and interest rates can spike.

Relationships, brand, and systems hold their value. Your portfolio travels with you. That is freedom made portable.

Conclusion: The Balance Sheet of the Future

Wealth once was counted in square footage. Soon, it will be counted in reach and reputation.

The invisible investor does not chase deeds. The invisible investor builds digital, relational, and intellectual equity that compounds for a very long time.

Your portfolio does not live in a filing cabinet. It lives in your ecosystem. When you learn to track it, to optimize it, and to grow it, you will never again depend on ownership to build wealth.

The richest people of the next decade will not be the ones who own the most. They will be the ones who control the most.

In the next chapter, you will take this idea to its endpoint and learn how to exit without entry. You will see how to sell, license, or transfer your invisible empire for tangible profit, even if you never technically "owned" it.

Exit without Entry

When most people imagine an "exit," they think of selling a building. They picture a closing table, a wire transfer, a settlement statement, and the satisfaction of a large check tied to years of ownership. In the traditional real estate world, the exit is the finale, the day when patience, risk, debt, and management finally pay off. You bought the property, held the property, dealt with the property, and then, eventually, sold the property. It is linear, slow, and deeply tied to capital.

Invisible investors navigate exits through an entirely different lens. Their exits rarely involve deeds, mortgages, or physical assets. Instead, their exits come from selling what they built around opportunities, the systems, brands, communities, partnerships, digital assets, intellectual property, operational engines, and influence. Their exits are not tied to the value of a single property but to the value of their architecture.

An invisible investor does not wait for appreciation; they create it. And when the time comes to exit, they are not exiting a building; they are exiting leverage.

This chapter is about those exits, the ones that do not require buying property, but instead require building something far more valuable.

The Paradox of the Invisible Investor

Most people assume you cannot sell what you do not legally own. The Invisible Investor proves you can sell the systems that create value, even when the deed sits elsewhere.

Ownership was the old gateway to wealth. In the present economy, defined by intellectual property, automation, and brand, control over repeatable systems is the true gateway to liquidity.

Those systems are transferable, and anything transferable is sellable. You do not need to own buildings to sell an empire when you own the infrastructure of influence.

The Myth That You Need to Own Something to Sell It

The traditional mindset says you must buy an asset to later sell it. Ownership precedes exit. But in the modern economy, ownership is no longer the main prerequisite for monetization. Today, you can exit a system you built even if you never owned the underlying property. You can exit a community you nurtured. You can exit a brand you developed. You can exit a set of digital assets that shape where capital flows.

Businesses are bought and sold every day without owning physical assets:

- Marketing firms sell for millions while owning no real estate.

- Social media brands exit for seven figures with no inventory.
- Lead generation companies sell for more than property portfolios.
- Consulting agencies sell based on their intellectual property and processes.
- Digital communities are acquired for their audience and engagement.

The invisible investor steps into this world not just as a participant but as a creator. Their portfolio is made of mechanisms, not buildings. Their sellable assets are intellectual, digital, relational, and operational. Because these assets are easier to transfer and faster to scale, their exits can be larger, sooner, and far more flexible than traditional property sales.

The New Definition of an Exit

For decades, exit meant selling a company or a portfolio of properties. Today, exits happen whenever a repeatable engine changes hands, whether that engine is a website, a data platform, or a recurring revenue contract.

A real exit occurs when your creation produces value for someone else without you. That is the essence of the invisible model.

You can exit from

- A digital brand.
- A lead generation system.

- A subscription or membership business.
- A network or data platform.
- A management company.
- A licensing or education product.

All without ever taking title to an asset.

Think of these as portfolios of rights and relationships, not piles of things.

Case Study: The Digital Brokerage Sale

A small team in Phoenix ran a digital brokerage under a national franchise. They built custom automation, customer relationship templates, and local search systems to generate inbound leads.

When they chose to pivot, they sold the entire digital backend rather than the legal entity.

A regional brokerage paid $650,000 for the funnels, templates, and database.

No physical transfer.

No escrow.

Just intellectual property changing hands.

They exited without entering traditional ownership.

Why Exiting Invisible Assets Works

Invisible assets are built on qualities that make them highly marketable. They are,

- Predictable through subscriptions, management fees, or automation.

- Portable because they carry no geographic limits and little physical infrastructure.
- Transferable because systems and data can be replicated or licensed quickly.

In essence, they behave like digital real estate that earns rent while appreciating in traffic, brand equity, and automation maturity.

Exiting Systems Instead of Structures

One of the most powerful types of exits for an invisible investor is the sale of a system. A well-built system, whether it is a lead funnel, an operational framework, a short-term rental automation suite, or a deal flow engine, has value precisely because it is functional without your constant involvement. If a system consistently produces cash flow, solves a problem, or creates opportunity, someone will gladly pay for it.

Imagine a Creator who builds a website that generates steady investor leads. Over time, this site becomes a digital asset with real monetary value. The Creator can sell it outright, lease it, license it, franchise it, or partner with someone who wants to scale it into new markets. They might exit the system entirely or keep a percentage of revenue in perpetuity.

Similarly, a Controller who has built a sophisticated operational model, complete with automation, pricing optimization, vendor management, and onboarding flows, can sell the operational blueprint to other operators. They can license it, replicate it across multiple markets, or sell the entire system to a property management company seeking modernization.

A Connector who has organized a powerful network can sell access rights, transition ownership of the network, or partner with someone who wants to expand the community into an enterprise-level platform. In each scenario, the system, not the property, is the asset. And that asset can have exit potential equal to or greater than the buildings it surrounds.

Case Study: The Education Platform Exit

A real estate coach built an online course that taught creative finance strategies. After five years, a community of 20,000 students generated more than $60,000 each month in recurring income.

When he moved on to new ventures, a proptech company purchased the brand and its membership rights for $2.5 million.

They did not buy his personal knowledge.

They bought distribution.

The systems, the audience, and the reputation were the assets.
He exited a digital classroom the way a developer exits a tower.

Exiting a Brand or Digital Presence

Today, a brand is often more valuable than a building. A brand can reach millions. A building can hold a handful. A brand can evolve; a building deteriorates. A brand can generate revenue in countless ways; a building has a fixed income ceiling.

Invisible investors who understand branding create assets that can be sold, licensed, or merged into larger platforms, for example:

- A real estate content brand with 100,000 email subscribers.
- A city-specific investor education hub with 20,000 monthly visitors.
- A niche short-term rental blog with optimized SEO rankings.
- A YouTube channel focused on creative finance.
- A podcast interviewing high-level operators.
- A social community with strong engagement.

These are exit-worthy assets. They have attention, trust, influence, and reach; exactly what real estate companies, brokerages, lenders, and tech startups will pay a premium to acquire.

A well-positioned Creator can exit their digital brand for a multiple of recurring revenue. A newsletter publisher can sell their list to an education company. A community leader can merge their group with another and receive compensation or equity. A YouTube channel can be sold outright or rolled into a media network. The invisible investor does not build digital assets for content's sake; they build them for exit potential.

The Hidden Market for Invisible Exits

Invisible exits happen quietly in niche markets that mirror real estate valuation principles.

Common Marketplaces

- Empire Flippers – Websites and digital brands (valued 30×–50× monthly profit).
- MicroAcquire (Acquire.com) – SaaS and online businesses.
- Flippa – Smaller lead-gen and e-commerce properties.
- BizBuySell – Service and subscription models.

Each platform functions like a listing service for invisible assets.
Buyers purchase systems, lists, and relationships that produce cash flow.

Exiting Partnerships and Profit Shares

Collaborators and Connectors often build partnerships that accumulate value over time. A Collaborator might contribute design, management, or consulting expertise to a property owner in exchange for a share of profits. Over time, those profit streams create predictable income, which can then be sold, much like selling a stake in a business.

In some cases, a Collaborator may act as an advisor to multiple developers, accumulating fractional shares across dozens of deals. These fractional equity positions can be packaged and sold to investors looking for recurring cash flow without operational responsibilities.

Connectors, similarly, may curate introductions for multiple operators, earning referral income or profit shares on deals. These revenue streams can also be packaged and sold, especially when supported by documented systems and established relationships. In both cases, the exit is not from owning property, but from orchestrating outcomes.

Exiting Communities and Networks

Communities are the new frontier of both wealth creation and wealth exit. Private memberships, mastermind groups, investor communities, and local meetups have become powerful leverage assets. As these communities grow in size and engagement, they become valuable acquisition targets for education companies, investment firms, brokerages, and technology platforms.

A well-run community becomes a brand. A brand becomes authority. Authority becomes value. And value becomes exit. Imagine a monthly investor group that grows to 2,000 members and produces consistent revenue through memberships, sponsorships, or events. The founder can sell the group outright, merge it with another community, or step into a strategic partnership where another operator runs it day to day.

For the invisible investor, communities represent a way to monetize years of influence without ever buying a building.

Exiting Technology, Tools, and Intellectual Property

In the digital age, every tool you create can become an asset someone else wants to buy:

- Deal calculators and underwriting models.
- Templates, frameworks, and scripts.
- Licensing contracts and legal packs.
- Automation tools and integrations.
- Operational manuals and SOP libraries.
- Content libraries and training programs.
- AI-based pricing or forecasting tools.
- Onboarding and qualification systems.

Invisible investors accumulate these tools naturally as they refine their models. Over time, the toolkit itself becomes something others are willing to pay for, either as a one-time purchase, a subscription, or a complete acquisition. A well-organized toolkit can sell for tens of thousands of dollars or more, especially when it comes with proof of performance.

Valuing Invisible Assets

Valuation is both an art and an algorithm. Here is how professionals price invisible empires.

Asset Type	Typical Multiple	Key Drivers
Digital Media / SEO Sites	30×–45× monthly profit	Traffic stability, organic growth

Asset Type	**Typical Multiple**	**Key Drivers**
Subscription / Memberships	3×–6× annual profit	Retention rate, churn, automation
Management Businesses	1×–3× annual revenue	Contracts, client diversification
Licensing / Education	2×–5× annual profit	Intellectual property, content depth
Data / Lead Platforms	4×–8× annual profit	Accuracy, engagement, renewal rates

What drives the multiple is system strength. The less the business depends on you personally, the higher the valuation. The Invisible Investor builds engines that others can operate on day one.

Framework: The Exit Readiness Test

- **Can it operate without me?**

  (If not, document and delegate.)

- **Can revenue be tracked and verified?**

  (Transparency builds buyer confidence.)

- **Is there recurring income?**

  (Predictability = premium valuation.)

- **Is the brand or data transferable?**

  (Ensure ownership of domains, IP, and lists.)

- **Is reputation independent of personality?** (Brand > Individual = scalability.)

If you can answer yes, you are exit-ready even if you have never owned a single property.

Case Study: The Management Company Rollup

A property management firm in Denver focused on short-term rentals. They built automated pricing, guest communication, and owner reporting.

Over time, the technology became more valuable than the contracts. When a national operator approached to buy them, the negotiation centered on software integration, not property count.

The acquisition closed at four times annual profit, a number more common in technology than in management.

They exited through system equity, not inventory.

Building an Exit Ready Empire

Here is how to prepare your invisible business for a sale, partnership, or licensing deal.

- Productize your process so buyers can see clear deliverables, standard pricing, and step-by-step procedures.
- Separate the brand from the individual so the equity lives in the system, not in your name.
- Automate everything you reasonably can because automation increases reliability and valuation.

- Document intellectual property with dated records of content, contracts, templates, and code.
- Build buyer relationships well before you need them so you have a warm path when timing is right.
- Diversify revenue streams across affiliate, subscription, and management so valuation is stable and attractive.

Case Study: The Local Platform Exit

A group of agents in Florida built a hyperlocal website that ranked for city-specific keywords. They monetized with sponsorships, lender ads, and local partnerships.

After five years, it generated $200,000 per year with minimal overhead. A national media company acquired the site for $900,000, which was 4.5x the annual earnings.

There was no inventory and no staff.

There was search equity and trust.

They exited from attention equity.

Licensing as a Soft Exit

Not every exit requires a sale. Licensing can generate exit-level income while you retain ownership.

You can license

- Brand and marketing templates to other professionals.
- Digital assets (courses, data sets, or playbooks).
- Management systems or pricing tools.

Think of it as a fractional exit income recurring, diversified, and fully scalable.

Example

A California operator licensed an Airbnb management system to 25 partners nationwide for $500 per month. That is $150,000 per year in mostly passive income while retaining ownership.

She exited her local workload while keeping the intellectual property.

The Invisible M&A Era

Mergers and acquisitions are no longer reserved for giant corporations.

Invisible investors participate in micro deals every month.

- Consultants merge databases.
- Agencies acquire newsletters.
- Property managers absorb smaller portfolios.

Each transaction is a miniature exit that democratizes wealth transfer. Invisible empires change hands and quietly build a new middle class of digital capitalism.

Case Study: The Podcast Exit

Two entrepreneurs hosted a podcast for real estate professionals.

They monetized with sponsorships and coaching funnels.

When listenership reached 8,000 downloads each

month, a national education brand purchased the show for $1.2 million for its audience and archives.

They did not own a product. They owned attention, access, and trust.

Their microphone became an asset.

Framework: The Invisible Exit Map

Stage	Objective	Example
Stabilize	Build recurring income and automation.	Management contracts, digital funnels.
Systemize	Document every process for replication.	SOPs, CRM workflows, scripts.
Brand	Establish an independent identity.	Logos, domain, authority, content.
Package	Organize deliverables for sale.	Data sets, dashboards, client lists.
Exit / License	Transfer or lease your systems.	Acquisition, franchise, or licensing.

This roadmap mirrors a development cycle. You build, stabilize, transfer, and repeat in the invisible realm.

Legal and Structural Considerations

Invisible exits still require strong legal frameworks.

1. **Intellectual Property Transfer Agreements:** Define ownership of domains, designs, content, and data.
2. **Non-Compete and Non-Solicitation Clauses:** Protect both buyer and seller.
3. **Revenue Continuity Clauses:** Outline transition periods to maintain client relationships.
4. **Tax Treatment:** Most digital asset sales are treated as capital gains, favorable compared to ordinary income.
5. **Advisory Support Periods:** Offer post-sale consultation to maximize goodwill and valuation.

A strong legal structure turns your invisible assets into tangible, saleable property.

The Emotional Side of Exiting

Exiting something you built requires mindset work.

You are not selling identity. You are freeing energy for higher opportunities.

Wealth flows to where attention goes. The ultimate luxury is attention freedom. That is the emotional dividend of invisible investing.

The Freedom of Exiting Without Ever Entering

The greatest advantage of invisible exits is that they are not locked to market cycles. A traditional investor must wait for the right moment to sell a property, navigating interest rates, pricing trends, buyer demand, and economic conditions.

Invisible investors can exit whenever they choose. A system can be sold at any time. A digital brand can be acquired at any time. A community can be merged at any time. An operational model can be licensed at any time. Influence does not rise and fall with the housing market; it rises and falls with value creation.

This freedom becomes a superpower. It gives the investor optionality, liquidity, and time. It gives them the ability to reallocate focus without waiting on a closing. And it allows them to build a legacy that is not tied to the fragility of a single building or a single market.

Case Study: Exit to Partnership

A consulting firm that built lead funnels for lenders chose a partnership rather than a full sale. The new structure paid 15% of national marketing profits while the parent company handled execution.

They did not walk away. They stepped up from operator to partner.

Labor equity became ownership equity.

Exit Timing: Knowing When to Let Go

Timing invisible exits uses a different compass.

- Sell or license when growth plateaus and a larger platform can take it further.
- Package and scale when replication works reliably in more than one market.

- Transition when passion shifts, so you move before burnout.

The best exits happen at peak potential. You sell the possibility with fuel still in the tank.

The Legacy of Invisible Empires

Every invisible investor reaches a crossroads. Scale or crystallize wealth.

Your systems, relationships, and brand can outlive you. They can be sold, licensed, or handed down. Legacy is not about paper deeds.

It is about continuity of influence. Your invisible empire is the infrastructure that others will build on.

Common Pitfalls and Red Flags

Do not promise outcomes that depend on your personal relationships if those relationships will not transfer. Do not hide single-channel risk where most traffic or revenue comes from one source. Do not mix personal and business accounts.

Clean separation protects value.

Conclusion: Profit without Possession

To exit without entry is proof that wealth is not confined to ownership. You can create, scale, and sell ecosystems built from knowledge, systems, and trust.

The modern investor does not need land to leave a legacy. The modern investor needs leverage. When you sell systems, license knowledge, or transfer influence, you convert control into capital.

That is the highest level of freedom. Because the Invisible Investor does more than build wealth.

The Invisible Investor creates liquidity from thin air.

In the next chapter, Chapter 11: The Ethical Edge, we will explore the boundaries of this new power, how to maintain trust, integrity, and transparency while operating in a world where control is more powerful than ownership.

The Ethical Edge

There is a silent truth woven through every chapter of this book, the invisible investor holds a different kind of power than traditional investors. It is not the power that comes from owning the deed. It is the power that comes from shaping outcomes, influencing markets, curating relationships, orchestrating opportunities, and guiding others through uncertain terrain.

With that power, comes responsibility. Influence, unlike property, is fragile. It is rooted in trust. It thrives on reputation. And it can disappear the moment integrity is compromised. Ethics are not a decorative layer in the invisible investor's model; they are the foundation.

Invisible investing operates in the relational realm. People choose you because they trust you. They follow your recommendations because you have earned credibility. They join your communities because they feel safe. They buy your systems because they believe you have tested them. They enter partnerships because they sense alignment. You are not leveraging buildings; you are leveraging belief. And belief must be protected.

This chapter explores the ethical architecture that keeps the invisible investor's empire stable. It shows why operating with integrity is not just the right thing to do; it is the most profitable long-term strategy. It explains how transparency acts as a growth multiplier, how collaboration becomes stronger when expectations are clear, and how influence becomes sustainable only when rooted in respect. Ethical leverage is not the opposite of strategic leverage; it is the highest form of it.

The New Frontier of Leverage

Every revolution needs a moral compass. In real estate, the old compass was simple.

If you bought it, you owned it. If you owned it, you controlled it. If you controlled it, you were accountable for it.

In the invisible economy, where control, data, and influence replace deeds, those lines blur.

You can shape markets without owning assets.

You can drive value without legal responsibility.

You can profit without possession.

That freedom creates risk. Carelessness, opportunism, and exploitation spread when incentives outpace governance.

To operate as an Invisible Investor is to wield power without abusing it. It's the difference between manipulation and mastery, between extraction and elevation.

Ethics is not a soft skill here. It is a competitive edge.

The Reputation Economy

In the invisible world, trust is currency. It shows up on your balance sheet as renewal, referral, and reach. When your business depends on access, influence, and community, reputation becomes both a moat and a multiplier.

You cannot hide behind property, title, or corporate infrastructure. The value you create lives in perception, and perception lives in receipts. One breach can erase years of credibility. Treat verification, documentation, and disclosure the way a landlord treats title.

Check it, protect it, and defend it.

Make the proof easy to see.

Publish how you earn, how you store data, and how you resolve complaints. The more your market knows, the less it needs to guess.

Why Invisible Power Requires Visible Responsibility

Traditional investors can hide behind their assets. If a landlord is difficult, the property still exists. If a developer cuts corners, the building still stands. If an owner disappears, the tenants remain. An invisible investor's wealth, by contrast, is tied directly to their reputation. If trust erodes, the entire structure collapses.

This creates a unique dynamic, invisible investors are more accountable to relationships than traditional investors are to properties. You cannot afford to be careless. You cannot afford to be vague. You cannot afford to be purely transactional. You cannot afford short-term wins that cost long-term credibility.

Your entire ecosystem, the one you have been building across these chapters, exists because people believe in you. That is the ethical edge, and it is what separates durable empires from short-lived schemes.

Case Study: WeWork and the Cost of Overreach

WeWork was one of the most ambitious control-based businesses ever built.

They did not own the buildings. They controlled them through master leases and resold the experience at a markup, the quintessential Controller model.

At its peak, WeWork had a **$47 billion** valuation. Then it collapsed almost overnight.

Why?

Because the company confused influence with entitlement. The leadership culture prioritized growth over governance, marketing over management, and hype over honesty. They blurred the line between vision and accountability.

The lesson is simple.

In a world built on control, ethics are the only guardrails strong enough to prevent self-destruction.

The Difference between Leverage and Exploitation

Leverage is the ability to create outcomes efficiently. It is built on alignment, consent, and mutual benefit. Exploitation is the extraction of value at someone else's expense. It is built on secrecy, misalignment, or pressure.

Invisible investors operate in a world where the line between leverage and exploitation can blur if not handled with clarity. A master lease, for example, gives an operator significant control over a property. Used properly, it helps both parties. Used improperly, it creates asymmetric risk for the owner. A referral agreement can bring opportunity to an investor but can feel manipulative if expectations are unclear. A community can be empowering or predatory depending on how information is presented.

The invisible investor must keep asking,

- Is this relationship mutually beneficial?
- Am I communicating clearly?
- Does everyone understand the risks?
- Am I leaving the other party better than I found them?

If the answer to any of these questions is "no," you are not leveraging, you are extracting. Extraction is profitable temporarily. Collaboration is profitable permanently.

The Invisible Investor Code of Conduct

To operate sustainably in this new paradigm, you need an internal compass, a framework that defines integrity in systems, not slogans.

1. Transparency

Be clear about your role, value, and incentives. If you profit from a referral, a marketing fee, or a partnership, disclose it.

Transparency transforms skepticism into trust. State what you earn, when you earn it, and what the counterparty receives in exchange.

2. Reciprocity

Never extract information without returning a value. Every introduction, lead, or collaboration should create mutual benefit.

Reciprocity is the invisible investor's gravity. It keeps relationships in orbit.

3. Accountability

Own the outcomes you influence, even when you do not own the asset. If your systems fail or your recommendations cause loss, take responsibility. Accountability builds long-term authority.

5. Authenticity

Operate in alignment with your actual expertise. Do not present yourself as a lender, agent, or developer if you are not. Authenticity compounds faster than pretense.

6. Sustainability

Choose long-term trust over short-term gain. Sustainable profits are built on consistency, not opportunism.

Fieldwork.

Convert these five principles into a one-page policy you can share in proposals and on your site. Visibility turns values into promises you can be measured against.

Transparency as a Growth Strategy

Transparency is often described as a virtue, but for the invisible investor, it is also a competitive advantage. Most people carry a low-level skepticism about real estate. They are used to fine print, hidden agendas, and half-truths. When someone operates with genuine transparency, it stands out immediately.

Transparent operators attract higher-quality partners. They are recommended more often. They negotiate from a position of trust. They scale faster because there is no reputational drag. Transparency accelerates opportunity rather than slowing it down.

You do not need to reveal every detail of your cost structure, but you do need to be clear about,

- What you bring to the table
- What the other party brings
- How value is created
- How outcomes are shared
- How conflicts will be handled

- What expectations exist
- Where the boundaries are

Invisible investors understand that clarity does not reduce leverage; it expands it.

Case Study: The Ethical Wholesaler

Wholesaling, assigning contracts for profit is one of the purest forms of invisible investing. You control property without owning it.

However, it is also the most abused.

Unlicensed operators sometimes mislead sellers, inflate buyer fees, or disguise intent.

Then a new standard emerged: transparent wholesalers.

Transparent wholesalers demonstrate value before they earn fees, and they protect both sides of the transaction. They lead with written disclosures, verifiable timelines, and documented capacity to close or to assign responsibly.

One example often cited is KeyGlee, a national wholesaling firm that grew by professionalizing a space known for informality. The model was simple and visible.

Their marketing explained the contracts and terms in plain language, showing sellers exactly how the wholesale price connects to the final disposition price, with no surprise line items at closing.

Buyers received complete packets with defined inspection windows, proof of equitable interest, and clear step-by-step instructions for deposits and cancellations.

What Ethical Wholesaling Looks Like In Practice

- Informed consent.

The seller understands that the agreement creates an assignable equitable interest. The assignment right is not buried in fine print. It appears near the signatures in plain language with a brief explanation.

- Real capacity.

The wholesaler documents funds or partner capacity before marketing the deal, and limits marketing to buyers who acknowledge the inspection and earnest money terms.

- Honest pricing.

The assignment fee is disclosed as either a fixed amount or a visible spread. If a spread is used, the wholesaler shows the offer that will be presented to the end buyer, so the seller is not surprised at closing.

- Shared safeguards.

Inspection periods, clear contingencies, and cancellation rights protect everyone. Sellers are not rushed into signing, and buyers are not trapped by undisclosed conditions.

KeyGlee did not win because assignment fees disappeared. It won because the fee became defensible. When both sides understand the role, the time saved, and the reach created, the premium feels like distribution value rather than arbitrage in the dark.

Why Trust Creates Compounding Leverage

Trust compounds like capital. It grows with each positive encounter, each fulfilled promise, each honest conversation. Over time, trust becomes its own form of equity. It makes introductions smoother, negotiations easier, and partnerships more enjoyable. It increases your earning potential without increasing your effort.

A single act of integrity can become the seed of a decade-long relationship. A single broken promise can end many. Invisible investors are not transactional; they are relational. They understand that the person they help today, even at no immediate benefit, may become a partner five years from now or may introduce them to someone who changes everything.

Real opportunities are rarely obvious upfront. They emerge from long-term momentum. Ethics are not just guardrails; they are the engine that keeps your network and deal flow compounding.

Ethical Leverage in Practice

Ethical leverage means structuring deals where everyone wins: owners, partners, clients, and you. It is not altruism; it is optimization.

Because in a reputation economy, your return on integrity always exceeds your return on investment.

Example:

A management company offers revenue share agreements with homeowners. Instead of charging flat fees, they align incentives; more profit for the owner means more profit for them. That is ethical leverage, alignment over exploitation. The invisible investor must design systems that make fairness profitable.

Ethics as a Market Differentiator

In a noisy marketplace full of hype, manipulation, and short-sighted tactics, the invisible investor stands out precisely because they refuse to operate that way. Their restraint becomes their branding. Their quiet competence becomes their marketing. Their consistency becomes their magnetism.

People do not follow invisible investors because they shout the loudest. They follow them because they feel safest around them. That is the strongest form of influence you can have.

The Real Cost of Cutting Corners

Every shortcut in the invisible economy carries a hidden cost. Being vague about your role makes people question your intentions. Overpromising leads to disappointment that kills momentum.

Manipulating someone into a partnership breeds resentment. Hiding risk exposes you to reputational damage. Taking advantage of someone's inexperience poisons your network. Trying to maximize every dollar minimizes your career longevity.

Invisible investing is not a one-time opportunity; it is a lifestyle. And lifestyles only last when they are built on principles, not tactics. Integrity is not optional. It is existential.

Framework: The Ethics Multiplier

Principle	Behavior	Result
Transparency	Openly disclose compensation and intent.	Builds trust and referrals.
Accountability	Take ownership of outcomes.	Strengthens authority.
Reciprocity	Ensure mutual value.	Creates collaboration networks.
Consistency	Deliver reliable results.	Stabilizes reputation equity.
Respect	Protect people's data, time, and dignity.	Expands long-term reach.

Each principle amplifies the others and converts behavior into brand equity.

Track these principles with simple metrics such as partner retention, dispute resolution time, and percent of contracts with written disclosures so ethics becomes an operating rhythm, not a slogan.

How Ethical Leadership Creates More Wealth over Time

Eventually, the invisible investor discovers something that sounds idealistic but proves mathematically true, ethics make you more money. Ethics create loyalty. Loyalty creates opportunity. Opportunity creates scale. Scale creates wealth.

The real estate world is full of people who burn bridges chasing short-term gains. Invisible investors patiently build bridges that last decades. They know that the best deals are rarely found; they are offered. And offers tend to flow toward the people with the cleanest reputations.

In the invisible economy, your name becomes your balance sheet. The clearer and cleaner it is, the higher your long-term valuation.

Case Study Zillow and Data Ethics

Zillow redefined access by giving consumers free visibility into property data once reserved for insiders. That transparency built massive user trust until Zillow blurred the line between platform and player with its failed iBuyer program.

When they began competing against their own clients, trust fractured. It was not about pricing errors; it was about perception of fairness. Users felt betrayed; the brand that empowered them was now profiting from them.

Zillow's stock price and reputation both suffered.

Lesson:

Transparency is powerful. But once broken, it is difficult to rebuild.

Marketplace operators can reduce this risk with a neutrality policy and equal data access rules that keep the platform from advantaging itself over participants.

The Law of Asymmetric Ethics

The more invisible your business, the more visible your behavior. Because your reputation is your brand, and your brand lives online, permanently.

In the digital world, integrity scales faster than deceit. A single screenshot or review can influence hundreds of potential partners. Every transaction, every message, every policy compounds in the public record.

Invisibility demands higher ethics, not less. Write and act as if every clause will be quoted in public, because one day it will.

The Paradox of Power

When you control but do not own, your ethical choices determine your durability. You cannot hide behind ownership contracts or assets.

Your entire enterprise rests on intangible capital, trust, systems, and access.

That means the smallest breach of ethics does not just hurt your image, it devalues your entire portfolio. Treat ethical lapses as asset impairments, publish the remedy, and time-bound the fix so stakeholders can see the repair, not only the apology.

Case Study Compass and the Culture of Trust

Compass, one of the fastest-growing brokerages in the world, did not succeed because of its technology alone; it succeeded because it sold a trust culture to its agents.

Their pitch was not more money, it was more partnership.
They built loyalty through shared values, transparency, collaboration, and design integrity.

As a result, agents became evangelists, not employees.

The brand's ethics became its engine. Service level commitments, documented marketing support, and clear agent payment timelines made promises measurable and repeatable.

The Invisible Investor Due Diligence Checklist

Before entering into any deal, ask.

Do I fully understand my impact? Am I influencing outcomes responsibly?

Is everyone aware of the terms? Since hidden clauses create future chaos

Would I be comfortable if this deal were public? If not, it is already unethical.

Does the structure reward fairness? Incentives reveal integrity.

Am I protecting the weaker party? True power safeguards, not exploits.

Run this checklist before every partnership, collaboration, or monetization. It is your compass in the gray zones of invisible leverage.

If feasible, add two more confirmations.

Is there a clean exit route for both sides? Is there a written remediation plan with owners and dates so problems have a visible path to resolution?

Consent Architecture

Ethical control begins with consent that is clear, granular, and revocable. Here is how to implement a robust and ethical control on consent.

Make consent visible.

Place data and referral disclosures where the action happens, not in a policy footer.

Make consent specific.

Separate boxes for email, SMS, and partner sharing. One box should equal one use.

Make consent reversible.

Every email, portal, or dashboard should include a one-click way to change preferences that actually works.

Record consent like revenue.

Store time stamps, channel, and policy version. Treat requests to delete as high-priority tickets with proof of completion.

Ethics and AI: The Next Dilemma

Artificial intelligence is transforming real estate, pricing models, underwriting, valuation, and content creation.

But AI introduces new ethical risks, bias, misinformation, and data misuse.

Invisible investors must treat AI as an amplifier, not a replacement for integrity.

Ethical AI means using verified data sources, disclosing when content or recommendations are machine-generated, and avoiding manipulative targeting or fabricated scarcity.

In a world of synthetic influence, authenticity becomes your last true differentiator.

To be on the safe side, always keep an audit trail of prompts and outputs for material decisions, run fairness tests on scoring models, and publish a short model summary that explains purpose and limits in plain language.

Case Study: Airbnb and Ethical Scaling

Airbnb began as a control-based success story, monetizing access, not ownership.

But as the company scaled, ethical dilemmas emerged, including city regulations, housing impact, and neighborhood backlash.

To sustain growth, Airbnb had to evolve from disruptor to responsible stakeholder.

They introduced host verification, safety protocols, and tax compliance systems.

The result?

Public trust returned, and with it, valuation stability. Airbnb proved that ethical infrastructure scales better than shortcuts.

Local compliance teams and consistent host standards turned a creative idea into a civic-grade service.

The Virtuous Cycle of Trust

Trust generates access.
Access generates opportunity.
Opportunity compounds wealth.
Wealth amplifies influence.
Influence, handled ethically, generates more trust.

That is the Virtuous Cycle of Trust, the most powerful compounding effect in invisible investing.

Every ethical action feeds back into your ecosystem, strengthening relationships, systems, brand, and capital.

You can measure the cycle with referral share, partner lifetime value, and complaint resolution time, so progress is visible and repeatable.

Framework: The Three C's of Ethical Leverage

C	Description	Application
Clarity	Communicate intentions and expectations openly.	Every contract and pitch.
Consent	Ensure all parties understand the exchange.	Data collection, partnerships, licensing.
Contribution	Create value that improves others' outcomes.	Collaboration and education initiatives.

These three form your ethical infrastructure.

Without them, control becomes corruption. Make consent reversible with a simple one-click mechanism, and log reversals as a health metric, not a nuisance.

Fair Claims and Honest Pricing

Publish the math behind your promise. If you claim a percentage lift, show baseline, period, inputs, and calculation method.

Quote the total cost of ownership, not teaser rates. Include platform fees, add-ons, and cancellation rules in the first view, not the last step.

Use testimonials with date, scope, and verification.

Remove results that are outliers or no longer representative.

Case Study: The Rise of B Corporations

B Corporations like Patagonia, Allbirds, and Ben and Jerry's have proven that ethical business models can outperform extractive ones.

In real estate, this mindset is emerging in firms that share profit with agents, create sustainable housing models, and prioritize diversity and local reinvestment.

Invisible investors can apply the same framework, aligning profit with purpose through equitable deal structures and transparent education.

Ethics scales faster when built into the system, not added as branding. A brief impact clause inside operating agreements gives partners a north star when tradeoffs appear.

The Cost of Ethical Debt

Just like financial debt accrues interest, unethical shortcuts accrue reputation debt. Each small compromise, an overstated claim, a delayed payment, a silent conflict, adds invisible liability.

Eventually, it compounds into loss of referrals, partnerships, or legal risk.

- The solution is simple.
- Pay ethical debt immediately.
- Resolve issues quickly.
- Communicate proactively.

It costs less to maintain trust than to rebuild it. It is also a good idea to hold a monthly ethics review that closes refunds, data requests, and service misses, then document fixes so errors do not repeat.

Long Term Leverage Integrity as Intellectual Property

Here is a truth many overlook: integrity is intellectual property.

When people know you operate fairly, your name becomes shorthand for reliability.

That is brand equity you cannot fake or buy. Integrity turns your reputation into an appreciating asset.

Every ethical decision is a deposit into your credibility bank, and it compounds exponentially.

Include your ethics playbook in proposals and onboarding so buyers see the operating standard before they sign.

Case Study: The Collaboration Economy

In the new economy, collaboration replaces competition. Brands like HubSpot, Notion, and Canva scaled globally by giving away tools and education free.

That generosity created ecosystems of loyal users, unpaid ambassadors.

Invisible investors can replicate this.

By freely sharing frameworks, resources, and introductions, you create network equity.

Network equity always pays dividends.

To begin, think of open-sourcing one non-core process to invite partners in, then earn participation through trust.

The Invisible Contract

Every deal you do, whether signed or unspoken, contains an invisible clause that "operates in good faith".

This unwritten contract binds the invisible economy together.

Because when you trade in access, data, and influence, legal enforcement is minimal, reputation is the only collateral.

Break that invisible contract, and you forfeit your most valuable asset, credibility.

The Ethical Legacy

Ethics is not about compliance. It is about continuity.

It is what ensures your systems, your brand, and your influence outlive you.

When your name becomes synonymous with fairness and quality, your empire keeps working long after you stop.

That is the ultimate invisible exit, legacy through trust.

Conclusion: The Highest Leverage of All

The invisible investor plays a long game. They know wealth without integrity is a short-term illusion.
Every deal, every message, every collaboration is a chance to multiply reputation or erode it.

The true secret of the invisible investor is not access or automation; it is ethics.

Because when your name becomes your asset, no market can take it away.

In the end, ethical leverage is the most powerful form of compounding wealth there is.

It turns influence into legacy. And legacy is the only ownership that truly lasts.

In the final chapter, Chapter 12: The Future of Ownership, we will look forward to what comes next: tokenization, decentralized assets, and the coming decade of invisible investing, where ownership, control, and identity converge into something entirely new.

The Future of Ownership

The world is entering a profound shift that will reshape how people build wealth, participate in markets, and interact with real estate. Ownership, once considered the pinnacle of financial achievement, is beginning to lose its centrality. For generations, owning property was synonymous with security. It was the primary path to long-term stability, the most visible marker of economic success, and the most celebrated milestone of adulthood. But cultural, technological, and economic forces are rewriting that narrative in real time.

The next decade will challenge almost everything people assume about what it means to be an investor. It will reward those who prioritize control over possession, access over acquisition, and agility over accumulation. The Invisible Investor is not an outlier; it is the early model of a future that is arriving faster than most people realize. In this new landscape, the Invisible Investor's model is not merely relevant; it is the blueprint.

Artificial intelligence, blockchain, digital identity, smart contracts, tokenization, fractionalization, dynamic pricing, and virtual marketplaces are not speculative trends. They are the new infrastructure of modern commerce. Real estate, historically slow to adopt technological change, is already integrating these innovations in ways that will completely reshape how wealth is built.

For the first time, individuals can participate in real estate without ever handling the property, qualifying for financing, or navigating the friction that once made ownership so burdensome. Access to information, once controlled by institutions, is now democratized. Tools once reserved for developers or institutional investors are becoming accessible to everyday operators. Data that was once expensive, incomplete, or difficult to interpret is now instant, comprehensive, and predictive.

The Ownership Illusion

For centuries, ownership defined success.

Land was wealth.

Property was permanent.

To own something meant to control it, and by extension, to control your destiny.

From medieval estates to modern mortgages, ownership promised security, legacy, and respect.

But ownership is changing.

What once signified freedom is now, in many cases, a liability, slow to move, expensive to maintain, and tied to institutions that no longer reward loyalty.

The next era of wealth will not be built by those who hold deeds.

It will be built by those who hold distribution. We are entering a world where access is the new ownership, and influence is the new capital.

The edge belongs to those who can redirect demand faster than an owner can refinance debt. When markets turn, control that moves at the speed of software will outrun assets that move at the speed of paperwork.

A Shift: 500 Years in the Making

To understand the future, look at the past. Every economic revolution redefined ownership:

- The Agrarian Era rewarded those who owned land.
- The Industrial Era rewarded those who owned factories.
- The Information Era rewarded those who owned data.
- The Access Era, our era, rewards those who own connections and control.

Just as electricity replaced steam, networked capital is replacing physical capital.

And just like industrial magnates built railroads to move goods, today's invisible investors build digital and relational infrastructure to move opportunity.

Each transition reduced the cost of participation and increased the premium on coordination. The winners were not those with the most stuff, but those with the best systems to route value.

In every turn, the scarce skill was orchestration. Today, orchestration looks like routing deals, attention, and capital across platforms with audit trails that others can verify.

The End of the Landlord Age

For the last century, property ownership was the surest path to wealth.

But the math has changed. Rising interest rates, regulatory friction, and compressed yields have eroded the margins of traditional landlords.

Owning property in 2030 looks very different than it did in 2010: more risk, less liquidity, and tighter compliance.

Meanwhile, new wealth classes, data owners, brand builders, and digital creators scale globally with near-zero overhead.

The industrial landlord owned the property.

The modern investor owns the platform.

That is not a downgrade. It is evolution.

The cash flow multiple once granted to buildings is migrating to software that drives bookings, pricing, and demand. In practice, the cap rate now sits on the system, not the structure.

The distinction between "owner" and "operator" is already blurring. Platforms now allow people to control assets through digital contracts, manage operations remotely, influence demand through pricing tools, and distribute returns automatically. In many models, the person who controls the system earns more than the person who owns the building. This is not theory; it is visible today in short-term rentals, flexible housing platforms, lease option marketplaces, and fractional investment networks.

From Tangible to Transferable

In the old model, power came from what you possessed.
In the new one, it comes from what you can transfer.

Transferability, the ability to replicate, license, or distribute, is now the highest form of value creation.

- Airbnb does not own rooms; it transfers access.
- Uber does not own cars; it transfers mobility.
- Amazon does not own most inventory; it transfers distribution.
- Modern investors do not own buildings; they transfer systems, knowledge, and influence.

Transferable assets are infinitely scalable.

They grow without physical boundaries.

They are the currency of invisible wealth.

The more portable the asset, the lower the friction to sell, exit, or partner, which raises valuation without adding weight.

In this new paradigm, what emerges is a different form of ownership, not based on possession but on participation. People will participate in real estate the way they participate in digital ecosystems, fluidly, flexibly, and repeatedly. They will hold stakes in multiple projects without the burden of managing them. They will earn revenue from digital assets that influence physical outcomes. They will trade control, information, and influence with the same ease they once traded stocks or commodities.

This shift rewards those who can see opportunity beyond the physical. For the Invisible Investor, the most valuable assets have always been intangible, systems, relationships, digital footprints, influence networks, operational frameworks, and intellectual property. These assets move faster than buildings. They scale easier than land. They respond instantly to market shifts.

The future of ownership is not about what you buy. It is about what you build.

Tokenization is the clearest expression of this change. Real estate tokens allow investors to buy and sell fractional interests with unprecedented liquidity. A ten percent stake in a multifamily project can be traded like a stock. Ownership becomes modular. Portfolios become flexible. The paperwork, waiting, negotiation, and friction of traditional transfers fade into the background as smart contracts handle the movement of value instantly. This fluidity mirrors what Invisible Investors have always sought, leverage without drag.

Case Study: Tokenized Real Estate

Blockchain technology introduced a new frontier, tokenization.
Tokenization fractionalizes ownership of real-world assets, buildings, developments, and even single-family homes into digital tokens that can be traded quickly.

Platforms like RealT, Lofty AI, and Ark7 already allow investors to buy micro shares in properties worldwide. For as little as $50, investors receive blockchain-verified ownership with distributed cash flow.

The result is liquidity and reach. You no longer need to own 100% of a property to participate in its upside.

You can own a fraction, trade it in seconds, and diversify globally.

Smart contracts can enforce waterfalls and investor rights with fewer intermediaries and fewer delays. The risk shifts from title friction to protocol risk, which means diligence moves from deeds to code and counterparties.

In this arena, the operator who curates quality deals becomes as important as the developer who pours concrete.

Decentralized Finance and Real Estate

Decentralized finance (DeFi) will play a monumental role in reshaping real estate wealth. Lending, borrowing, liquidity pools, staking mechanisms, and yield-generating protocols are already beginning to merge with property-based investments. Individuals will be able to collateralize digital assets to invest in physical properties. Rental income may be distributed directly into digital wallets. Smart contracts will replace layers of middlemen, reducing cost and increasing transparency.

This decentralization removes many of the barriers that once kept people from participating in real estate. Traditional gatekeepers, banks, institutional landlords, and legacy investment firms will lose their exclusive control. Individuals who understand how to navigate these technologies will access opportunities that once felt out of reach.

The Rise of the Decentralized Investor

Decentralization does not just change what we own. It changes who controls value.

In traditional real estate, power sits with banks, brokers, and governments. In the decentralized economy, power moves to networks of individuals who collaborate without intermediaries.

Imagine

- Crowdsourced developments funded through tokenized syndicates.
- Smart contracts automating rent, escrow, and profit sharing.
- Transparent public ledgers begin to replace title companies.

Decentralized ownership is trust through code.

It removes friction, and with it, unnecessary gatekeepers. The invisible investor thrives here because they already understand leverage without possession.

Community becomes capital when governance is clear and incentives are honest. The best sponsors will publish live dashboards so investors can see cash flow, occupancy, and risks in real time.

Simple governance works best. One token, one vote for policy, delegated committees for operations, and a public incident log so the community sees how problems are handled.

Case Study: Propy and the Smart Contract Closing

Propy, a blockchain-based real estate platform, has executed digital property transfers, including a United States home sold as an NFT.

Through smart contracts, buyers and sellers exchange verified documents, funds, and ownership records quickly and transparently.

This is the direction of ownership, borderless, frictionless, and paperless. As Web3 matures, these technologies will normalize.

Tomorrow's closings will feel like sending an email, and invisible investors will operate comfortably in that realm long before traditional players catch up.

The practical win is cycle time, fewer signatures, fewer back office errors, and clearer audit trails.

Before you digitize, create a three-item compliance pack.

Identity verification proof, source of funds proof, and consent logs for every upload and signature.

That pack lowers risk and speeds bank review.

Artificial Intelligence and Predictive Equity

Artificial intelligence is transforming operations even faster than most people realize. Intelligent systems now analyze neighborhoods, price properties, identify arbitrage opportunities, optimize short-term rental rates, streamline maintenance workflows, and evaluate risk with greater accuracy than many humans.

The Invisible Investor who leverages AI operates with the precision of a large institution but with the agility of a solo entrepreneur. They can scale across markets without being physically present, build influence across digital platforms without a massive team, and interpret data in real time.

In the next decade, ownership will become predictive, based on data-driven projections rather than static records. AI-driven valuation models already outperform many human appraisers in speed and accuracy.

Next-generation platforms will not only price assets, they will allocate capital autonomously.

For example, an AI fund could analyze short-term rental data, predict future yields, and automatically lease or sublet properties for profit without ever owning them.

Invisible investors who understand AI will build and lease digital operators instead of buildings. The new landlord will be an algorithm, and the new investor will be its architect.

The Rise of the Hybrid Economy

The future is not ownership or control. It is both.

Hybrid models will dominate, with partial ownership, full control, and distributed revenue.

Think of it like this: a developer tokenizes a property, a management company operates it under a smart contract, a marketing group controls digital demand funnels, and investors share returns automatically.

Each party holds invisible equity, ownership through function, not just paperwork.

This is decentralized syndication, real estate as an ecosystem, not only an asset class.

Write the split rules into code, then publish them in plain English so every party knows how value moves. When roles are transparent, velocity increases and disputes fall.

Case Study: Sonder and the Control Economy

Sonder built a billion-dollar hospitality brand without owning hotels.

They mastered the art of control without heavy capital, leasing buildings on long terms and transforming them into tech-enabled lodging experiences.

As AI and automation evolve, similar models will emerge across housing, retail, and logistics businesses that monetize operations and brand instead of walls and roofs.

Sonder proved that the next generation of empires will be built on experience control, not ownership scale.

The Metaverse Parallel

While physical real estate evolves, a parallel universe is forming. Digital real estate is no longer a metaphor; it is a market.

Platforms like **Decentraland, The Sandbox**, and **Spatial.io** allow users to buy, sell, and develop digital land. Major corporations, from Adidas to Sotheby's, have staked virtual claims.

To traditional investors, this can sound absurd. To invisible investors, it is familiar, leverage, access, and branding without tangible property.

Digital real estate operates on the same principles: scarcity, visibility, and utility.

The only difference is dimensional. Tomorrow's investors will diversify between physical and digital portfolios and manage both through unified dashboards and smart contracts.

The Emergence of Influence Equity

As digital ecosystems grow, influence is becoming measurable, tradable, and collateral. Platforms like Karat, CreatorDAO, and Rally already let creators monetize and tokenize it.

In real estate, agents, marketers, and educators will do the same by collateralizing personal brands and selling small stakes in audience or future revenue, turning reputation into an investable asset.

This is influence equity, the monetization of trust. For the invisible investor, influence equity is both currency and collateral.

Framework: The New Asset Classes of Invisible Wealth

Asset Type	Description	Example
Access Equity	Monetized networks and communities.	Memberships, masterminds, referrals.
System Equity	Processes and automation IP.	CRMs, funnels, and AI tools.
Brand Equity	Authority and audience monetization.	Sponsorships, tokenized influence.
Data Equity	Information and analytics value.	Market dashboards, predictive models.

Asset Type	Description	Example
Hybrid Ownership	Tokenized or fractional real assets.	Smart contracts, RE tokens.

Together, these assets form the backbone of invisible wealth, portable, scalable, and compounding. A mature portfolio blends all five, so no single risk can freeze your cash flow.

The Investor as Ecosystem Architect

In the past, investors optimized properties. In the future, they will optimize ecosystems.

An ecosystem investor does not just hold assets; they orchestrate people, platforms, and processes.

The portfolio spans

- Communities that generate deal flow,
- Brands that generate attention,
- Systems that automate delivery, and
- Partners who multiply opportunity.

Each element feeds the next.

That is why the invisible investor is the architect of tomorrow's economy, designing flows of value rather than hoarding static ones.

Case Study: Blackstone's Invisible Reach

Blackstone is one of the largest real estate owners in the world, yet its power lies not in its holdings, but in ecosystem control.

It manages more than one trillion dollars in assets, but its dominance comes from data integration, institutional relationships, and financial engineering.

Blackstone's ownership is often synthetic, held through partnerships, funds, and management structures rather than direct title.

They mastered invisible investing at an industrial scale, proof that the biggest landlords in history can also be invisible.

The Generational Divide

Millennials and Gen Z are redefining wealth on their own terms. They value flexibility over permanence, experiences over possessions, and digital reach over physical footprint.

Homeownership rates for these generations are historically low, not always because they cannot buy, but because they do not need to. They invest through side hustles, communities, and digital assets instead. For them, the invisible portfolio is not an alternative. It is the default.

The next twenty years will see power shift from property owners to presence owners. The best move is to learn compliance and stewardship early, so your reach compounds into reputation, not regret.

The Invisible Nation

Invisible investing is not only a financial model.

It is a social shift. It decentralizes opportunity, redistributes wealth, and dissolves gatekeepers.

- A 22-year-old in Bali can manage Airbnbs in Texas.
- A designer in London can profit from leads in Miami.
- A developer in Lagos can tokenize property in Dubai.

Geography is no longer destiny. Access, skill, and creativity are.

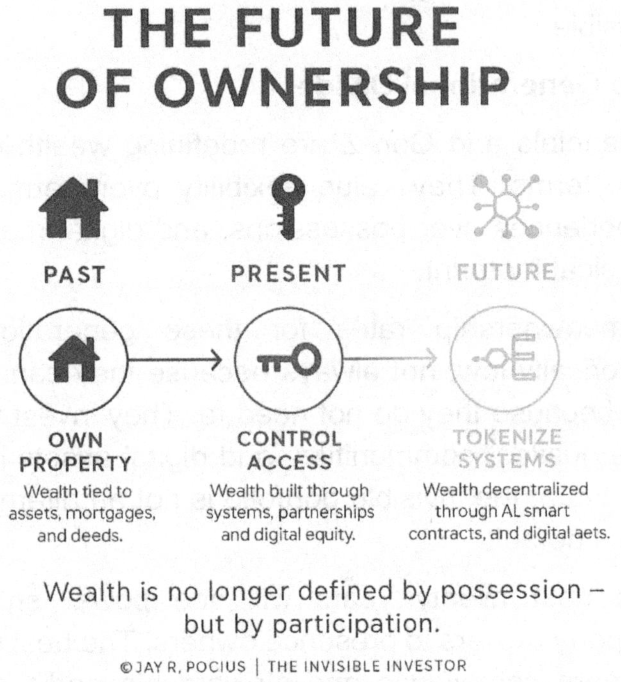

The invisible investor does not need permission to participate in the global economy.

They need Wi Fi and a framework.

Framework: The Future of Ownership Pyramid

Level	Ownership Type	Primary Leverage	Example
Physical Ownership	Traditional real estate and assets.	Capital.	Landlord, developer.
Digital Ownership	Domains, data, IP.	Attention.	Content, platforms.
Tokenized Ownership	Blockchain and smart contracts.	Transparency.	RealT, Propy, Lofty.ai.
Collaborative Ownership	Shared ecosystems and networks.	Trust.	DAO communities, joint ventures.
Invisible Ownership	Systems, influence, control.	Ethics + Innovation.	The Invisible Investor.

Each level is more fluid, scalable, and accessible than the last.

Every invisible investor can climb this pyramid one leverage layer at a time.

The safeguard across levels is governance; if incentives are clean, scale is safe.

The Ethical Imperative of the Future

Technology accelerates everything, including mistakes. As wealth creation becomes frictionless, the ethical edge from the last chapter becomes even more vital.

In the invisible economy, power concentrates around influence, and influence without accountability is dangerous. That is why the future of ownership must also be the future of responsibility.

- Transparency through blockchain.
- Fairness through smart contracts.
- Sustainability through tokenized accountability.

Ownership will no longer mean control over property. It will mean stewardship over systems. Publish your rules, publish your results, and publish your remedies when things go wrong.

From Wealth to Stewardship

True ownership, the kind that lasts, is not about possession. It is about preservation and participation.

Tomorrow's greatest investors will be custodians of ecosystems, not empires. They will create platforms where others can grow, profit, and collaborate.

That is how invisible investors create visible impact, through systems that outlive them.

Case Study: Regenerative Ownership

New ventures like ReFi DAO (Regenerative Finance) are using blockchain to fund environmental projects, carbon offsets, and community initiatives.

Investors earn yield not by extraction, but by contribution. They own impact.

This represents the ultimate evolution of ownership, turning capital into a catalyst. It is invisible wealth with a visible purpose.

When returns are tied to restoration, community trust compounds as quickly as capital.

The Legacy of the Invisible Investor

Ownership is no longer defined by boundaries, paperwork, or possession. It is defined by contribution, connection, and control of value flow.

Invisible investors are the architects of this transition, pioneers of a post-ownership world where wealth is measured not by what you have, but by what you create, enable, and sustain.

- Their empires are borderless.
- Their assets are digital.
- Their impact is tangible.

Legacy is what continues working for others when you are no longer in the room.

There will still be people who own buildings, and ownership will always have its place. But ownership will no longer be the only, or even the primary, path to wealth. Many investors will discover that controlling demand, operations, access, or influence can produce greater returns than holding the deed. Many will choose to own less because owning less gives them more freedom. And many will discover that the invisible routes to wealth, those that rely on creativity instead of credit, create the kind of life flexibility that traditional ownership rarely provides.

In the era ahead, investors who cling to the old definitions of wealth may feel left behind. They will wait for appreciation while others build systems. They will cling to property while others control the platforms that influence property. They will celebrate the accumulation of units while others celebrate the accumulation of leverage.

Those who adopt the Invisible Investor's mindset, resourceful, strategic, digital first, and collaboration driven, will thrive. They will stay light while others grow heavy. They will stay flexible while others become rigid. They will stay innovative while others cling to tradition. They will build wealth through access, participation, and influence, and they will embody the future long before the rest of the world realizes it has changed.

The next decade will belong to those who understand that ownership is optional, but leverage is essential. For the Invisible Investor, leverage is effectively unlimited.

Conclusion: The Great Unbundling of Wealth

The invisible investor is not a dreamer. They are a designer.

They do not escape ownership. They evolve it.

They understand that the most valuable assets of the 21st century cannot be held. They must be built, scaled, and shared.

The deed is declining. The ecosystem is rising.

And the investors who learn to operate without ownership, who influence, structure, and distribute value, will not only thrive in the future economy; they will define it.

Because the real power of invisible investing is not in what you control. It is in what you create for others, and in the legacy that continues long after you let go.

Epilogue: The Power of Not Owning

The Quiet Revolution

Every generation has its quiet revolution. Ours just happens to be invisible. For centuries, we were taught that ownership was the ultimate destination.

You worked, you saved, you bought the home and the car, and that proof of possession meant you had arrived. But somewhere along the way, the math stopped working.

The cost of ownership began to outweigh its rewards. The more we owned, the less we seemed to control. What started as a financial problem became a philosophical one.

If everything you own owns a piece of you in return, your time, your attention, your options, then maybe freedom does not come from owning.

Maybe it comes from designing systems so you can achieve actual freedom. That realization changed everything for me. And it is changing the world for a new generation of investors.

The quiet part is practical. Design systems that move value without dragging you with them, measure how fast they move, then remove anything that slows them down.

When motion compounds, freedom compounds with it. The shift is not anti-asset. It is pro-agility.

When outcomes depend on speed and proof, the lightest structure that still earns trust wins.

The Shift from Accumulation to Architecture

When people first hear about invisible investing, they assume it is about doing less. It is not. It is about designing smarter.

Ownership builds walls. Control builds bridges.

Owning means you are the landlord of a single building. Controlling means you are the architect of an entire skyline, and you can redesign it whenever the world changes.

In every deal, every partnership, every system, the invisible investor asks a different question. How can I add value without adding weight? That is not detachment, it is design.

It is the same principle that powers the modern world, clouds replacing servers, platforms replacing factories, access replacing possession.

We live lighter now, and we can move faster because of it. Since lightness turns setbacks into pivots, you can reconfigure the system quickly and keep momentum when conditions change.

Architecture replaces accumulation because it scales coordination and storage stalls. A single process that others can run becomes more durable than a single asset that only you can maintain.

The blueprint becomes the product when the outcome is reliable and the handoff is simple. That is why your real portfolio is a stack of decisions that anyone on your team can repeat.

If you can teach it in an hour and measure it in a day, you can scale it in a month. If you can change it without pausing the business, you can defend it for years.

Accumulation ties your identity to what you hold. Architecture ties your identity to what you enable.

The Weight of the Keys

Ownership is heavy. It is keys, maintenance, mortgages, insurance, taxes, and legal documents stacked high enough to block the view.

Invisible investors trade keys for codes, digital ones that unlock systems instead of doors.

They do not measure progress by square footage or inventory.
They measure it by velocity.

- How fast does value move through their ecosystem?
- How frictionless does the opportunity become?

When you design for velocity, you realize the best investments are not static; they are living systems that grow while you sleep.

Just as a key can be lost, copied, or withheld. A code can be rotated, logged, and shared with precision.

A heavy portfolio forces you to say no to new chances because your calendar belongs to your upkeep. A light portfolio lets you say yes with clarity because your time belongs to your best ideas.

That trade changes the slope of your life.

The Lesson of the Empty Office

I once toured a downtown office tower owned by a proud local investor. He walked me through twenty stories of glass and granite, explaining the rent roll and build-out costs in loving detail.

Then I asked a simple question.

How much time do you actually spend here? He laughed. Almost none.

That tower was a monument, impressive, immovable, and quietly exhausting. He spent more time managing the headaches of ownership than enjoying the fruits of it.

Two floors below, a startup rented a small suite in the same building.

Five people, no assets, all laptops.

They were earning more profit than the landlord who owned the place.

Same building.

Two models.

Two futures.

The difference?

One owned space.

The other owned systems.

The landlord carried a risk that did not translate to control. The start-up carried control that did not require risk.

The landlord priced in vacancies and repairs. The startup up priced in learning and speed.

The landlord optimized for occupancy. The start-up optimized for outcomes.

One path demanded capital before clarity. The other path demanded clarity before capital.

When markets shifted, the lease could be renegotiated in days, while the debt could not. That is the uneven physics of modern value.

Freedom through Design

When you release the need to own everything, you discover the freedom to design anything.

You can collaborate without competition, build partnerships without ego, and scale without debt.

You can turn ideas into income streams faster than most people can schedule a closing.

That does not make ownership obsolete. It makes it optional. And options are the true currency of freedom.

The Invisible Investor is not anti-ownership. They are post-ownership. They understand that the purpose of owning was never possession; it was control, security, and legacy.

But now, we can create those outcomes through other means, systems, technology, and shared access.

Design is a contract with your future self.

Choose structures that you can pause, transfer, or license without drama. If the only path out is a sale, you do not own options; you own obligations.

The Paradox of Control

It is ironic, the less you try to own, the more control you gain.

Ownership locks you in.

Control lets you pivot.

Every mortgage limits flexibility.

Every title ties you to maintenance.

Every deed slows momentum.

But a system?

You can duplicate it, license it, automate it.

It scales across time zones and industries.

Invisible investors do not escape responsibility; they redesign it. They take the same diligence required to buy property and apply it to buying freedom.

Because the ultimate asset is not the building, it is the blueprint and real control.

When your control is coded into the process, other people can improve it without breaking it. When your control lives in culture, new teammates protect it without being told.

That is how you move from personal effort to institutional rhythm. That is how you scale trust.

The Return on Lightness

In traditional investing, we talk about return on investment.
Invisible investors chase a different metric, return on lightness.

Lightness measures how much output you generate per unit of responsibility. It asks: How much income, impact, or influence can you create without additional weight.

The lighter you operate, the more responsive you become.
Lightness compounds like interest, freeing bandwidth for new opportunities while competitors drown in upkeep.

The richest people of the next decade will not be those with the most assets.

They will be those with the lightest leverage.

Legacy without Locks

Legacy used to be a will, a deed, a family business passed down like a sacred burden. Today, legacy can be a system, a network, or an idea that generates value long after you have moved on.

A digital course, a marketplace, a brand, a DAO, a data platform, all can outlive their creator.

They do not need maintenance; they need momentum. Invisible investors do not pass down property; they pass down playbooks. And playbooks are borderless.

That is the real inheritance of this era, transferable wisdom encoded in systems.

Case Study: The Platform That Outlived Its Founder

When Tony Hsieh built Zappos, he was not selling shoes; he was designing culture. When he passed away, Zappos did not collapse; it thrived because the system was bigger than the man was.

That is legacy without locks. The invisible investor builds frameworks that survive personality. They architect trust, process, and collaboration, the true building materials of permanence.

Culture became the product because service rules were clearer than style rules. Hiring rewarded kindness and curiosity as much as skill. Decision rights were documented so authority did not vanish when leaders were away.

The company sold certainty to customers by selling clarity to employees. That is why the platform endured.

People knew what to do next.

The Emotional Side of Not Owning

Letting go of ownership is not just financial; it is emotional. We equate ownership with identity. Selling the house, closing the company, delegating the work, it can feel like losing part of yourself.

In part, the fear is real because ownership is visible and validation is public.

The cure is practice, small releases that prove your life gets lighter when your grip softens. Delegate one process and measure the time you recover.

License one asset and measure the reach you gain. Share one playbook and measure the partners who arrive.

Identity grows when it is used in the service of others. Identity shrinks when it is spent on maintenance.

Abundance without Attachment

The invisible investor plays a different game of abundance.
They do not compete for slices of the pie; they design the bakery.

They know that the more people you empower, the more leverage you gain. Because access breeds opportunity, and opportunity shared is opportunity multiplied.

Attachment limits scale.

Contribution accelerates it.

When you operate from contribution, your network becomes self-sustaining. Partners promote you; clients defend you, and opportunities chase you.

That is the compounding effect of generosity, wealth through impact, not inventory.

Contribution, however, in no terms, means charity. It means building public goods that lower friction for your entire market.

It means answering the question that everyone asks and leaving the answer where everyone can find it. It means creating standards that competitors follow because it makes the whole category stronger.

In time, the market pays the person who made the work easier for everyone else. The brand you earn this way cannot be copied. It can only be matched by more contributions.

Case Study: The Community Multiplier

When BiggerPockets opened its forum to everyday investors, many professionals criticized the move. Why give away insider knowledge, they asked. But that transparency built a global ecosystem worth tens of millions annually.

The calculators turned anxiety into action. The podcasts turned strangers into regulars. The events turned avatars into allies. Each layer supported the next, and the whole stack produced more value than any single gatekeeper could.

By sharing value, they created infinite leverage. Their business grew precisely because they did not hoard ownership of information.

They distributed it, and in return, the community rewarded them with trust, attention, and revenue.

The Invisible Empire Within Reach

What does this mean for you?

It means you already have more leverage than you think.

- Every contact in your phone is a potential access to equity.
- Every process you have refined is potential system equity.
- Every idea you have shared is potential brand equity.
- Every community you have helped build is potential relationship equity.

You do not need permission, capital, or credentials to start building your invisible empire. You just need to look at your world differently, to see the assets that were always there.

The Future Belongs to Builders, Not Owners

Look ahead.

By 2035, more than half of the world's top one thousand companies will own fewer hard assets than their predecessors in 2020.

Software, systems, and ecosystems will outperform factories, fleets, and land holdings. In this future, the invisible investor is not an anomaly; they are the winners.

- They will publish how money moves before they ask for it.

- They will separate the brand from the person, so the platform lives longer than the founder.
- They will carry code, contracts, and communities that plug into new markets in days, not months.

Owners will still matter, but orchestration will decide margins. But the people who profit most will not be the ones with the most deeds; they will be the ones who build the pipelines of trust and distribution around those deeds.

They will be the ones who learned the power of not owning.

The Invisible Creed

If there is a creed to this new era, it might sound something like this.

- I design value I do not have to hold.
- I build systems that serve others and reward me in return.
- I measure wealth in freedom, not square footage.
- I trade ownership for influence, and possession for possibility.
- I leave spaces better than I found them.
- And I own nothing fully, yet I control everything that matters.

That is the invisible investor's philosophy in a single breath.

The Return to Human Capital

For all the technology and talk of automation, the invisible future is still human at its core.

People remain the ultimate platform. Every algorithm, every funnel, every tokenized system still depends on trust between individuals.

The best investors of the future will not be coders or financiers; they will be communicators.

Why? Because

Communication sets expectations, and expectations set margins.

Clear words reduce refunds. Clear promises reduce churn.
Clear boundaries reduce burnout.

Machines can route information, but only people can grant confidence. When confidence is present, deals move faster and disputes end sooner.

Speak plainly, document outcomes, and keep your word. That is the protocol that never goes out of date.

And the invisible investor never forgets that.

The Peace in Simplicity

There is a quiet peace in not owning.

You sleep lighter.

You move faster.

You focus sharper.

Your wealth does not live in storage units or spreadsheets; it lives in motion. And motion, when designed intentionally, becomes momentum.

That momentum is your real estate, the space you occupy in the minds, hearts, and systems of others.

Simplicity gives you back your mornings and protects your evenings. It gives you the margin to think, and thinking is still the strongest leverage you can own.

A Final Framework Freedom Flow

Freedom = (Value Created × Leverage Retained) ÷ Weight Carried

Create more value.

Keep more leverage.

Carry less weight.

If you created value but did not retain leverage, improve your terms. If you retain leverage but carry too much weight, redesign or delegate. If you carry little weight but create little value, invest in learning and in reach. The numerator feeds your pride, but the denominator decides your peace.

That is the invisible investor's equation for life. It is wealth through velocity, impact through lightness, ownership through purpose.

The Invitation

If this book has done its job, you no longer see real estate or wealth the same way.

You see opportunities where others see limits.

You see systems where others see walls.

You see equity in effort, income in insight, and legacy in leverage.

And maybe most importantly, you see that you do not have to own to belong.

The invisible investor is not a secret society. It is a mindset, available to anyone willing to build with intention, share with integrity, and design with purpose.

Start now.

- Choose one system to design lighter, offer a clear result, a clear timeline, and a clear split.
- Publish the outcome so the next partner arrives ready.
- Replace secrecy with standards and watch your pipeline change shape.

The work you are proud to share is the work that multiplies. That is how belonging turns into momentum.

The Closing Thought

Ownership used to mean security. Today, it often means inertia.

The world is moving faster than titles can transfer.

And the people who will thrive in the decades ahead are those who understand that true power lies not in possession, but in participation.

So as you close this book and open your next chapter, remember.

You can build wealth without buying it.

You can create legacy without locking it down.

You can control outcomes without controlling others.

Because the most valuable things in life, trust, time, creativity, and freedom, were never meant to be owned.

They were meant to be used, shared, and multiplied. And that is the real power of not owning.

Use it well, then pass it on.

Appendices

Appendix A — Sample Master Lease and Partnership Templates

Practical frameworks to help you structure invisible-investor deals safely, legally, and profitably.

Section 1: Master Lease Agreement (Short-Term or Multifamily Units)

Sample Contract Language

MASTER LEASE AGREEMENT
This Master Lease Agreement ("Agreement") is made and entered into as of [Date], by and between [Property Owner Name] ("Owner") and [Operator Name] ("Operator").

1. Property
Owner hereby leases to Operator the property located at [Address] ("Premises") for the purpose of operating short-term or mid-term rentals, subject to the terms of this Agreement.

2. Term
The term of this Agreement shall commence on [Start Date] and continue for [X years], with renewal options upon mutual consent.

3. Rent
Operator shall pay Owner a fixed monthly rent of $[Amount], due on the first day of each month. Owner shall have no entitlement to revenue generated from short-term rental operations, except as otherwise agreed herein.

4. Revenue Share (Optional Clause)
In addition to fixed rent, Operator agrees to pay Owner a

percentage of monthly net operating profit ("NOP") exceeding $[Threshold], at a rate of [__]%.

5. Maintenance & Utilities

The operator shall be responsible for interior maintenance, cleaning, and utilities related to operations. The owner remains responsible for major structural, roof, and system repairs.

6. Insurance

Operator shall maintain general liability insurance with coverage of no less than $1,000,000 per occurrence, naming Owner as additional insured.

7. Legal Compliance

Operator shall comply with all local laws, permits, and regulations governing rental operations, including licensing, occupancy, and tax remittance requirements.

8. Indemnification

Operator agrees to indemnify and hold harmless Owner against any claims, losses, or damages arising from Operator's rental operations, except for Owner's gross negligence.

9. Termination

Either party may terminate this Agreement with [X days] written notice for breach, or upon mutual consent.

10. Entire Agreement

This Agreement represents the entire understanding between the parties and supersedes any prior oral or written agreements.

Signed:

______________________________ (Owner)
______________________________ (Operator)

Plain-English Commentary

- **Purpose:** This structure lets you control income-producing property without owning it.
- **Key leverage:** Operator controls operations and cash flow while limiting liability.
- **Revenue share clause:** Adds flexibility, turns a pure lease into a partnership-style profit arrangement.
- **Risk management:** Insurance and indemnification are critical to protect both parties.
- **Compliance:** Always verify local laws; some municipalities require master lease disclosure for subleasing.

Section 2: Profit-Sharing Clause Between Operators and Owners

Sample Clause

"Operator shall remit to Owner 20% of monthly Net Operating Profit ("NOP"), defined as gross rental income less operating expenses, maintenance, utilities, and platform fees. Such payment shall be made by the 10th of each month, accompanied by a monthly financial statement."

Plain-English Commentary

- **Flexibility lever:** Aligns interests. The owner gets upside without management, the operator earns more when they perform.
- **Transparency:** Always define "Net Operating Profit" explicitly to avoid disputes.
- **Optional security:** You can pair this with a base rent floor for guaranteed minimum payments.

Section 3: Consulting-for-Equity Agreement (Collaborator Model)

Sample Agreement Outline

CONSULTING-FOR-EQUITY AGREEMENT

This Agreement ("Agreement") is entered into on [Date] by and between [Company Name] ("Client") and [Consultant Name] ("Consultant").

1. Purpose

Client engages Consultant to provide services in the area of [marketing, management, development, design, etc.].

2. Compensation

In lieu of or in addition to cash compensation, Client agrees to issue Consultant a [__]% equity interest in [specific property, project, or entity].

3. Vesting Schedule

Equity shall vest over [12/24 months] or upon completion of defined project milestones.

4. Performance Clause

Consultant's continued contribution and delivery of agreed milestones are required for vesting.

5. Profit Distribution

Consultant shall be entitled to [__]% of net distributable profits corresponding to their equity share, paid quarterly.

6. Exit Rights

Consultant's equity may be converted to cash value upon sale, refinance, or buyout of the underlying asset.

7. Confidentiality

Both parties agree to keep business terms and project data confidential.

8. Governing Law

This Agreement shall be governed by the laws of [State].

Plain-English Commentary

- **When to use:** Ideal for contractors, designers, marketers, or consultants trading value for long-term participation.
- **Vesting clause:** Protects both sides, ensures performance before full ownership.
- **Exit rights:** Clarify buyout terms upfront.
- **Tax note:** Always consult a CPA; equity-for-services can be taxable as ordinary income.

Final Note on Legal Compliance

These templates are educational examples, not legal advice. Always consult an attorney licensed in your state before executing agreements. Use these as starting frameworks to structure aligned, ethical, and compliant partnerships.

Appendix B — Lead Generation Funnels and Digital Asset Models

Blueprints for turning digital presence into profit, the invisible investor's "online property portfolio."

Section 1: Real-Estate SEO Site Structure

Blueprint Overview

A modern "digital real-estate" site is not a brochure; it's an ecosystem that attracts, converts, and recycles traffic into leads.
The ideal SEO architecture has three tiers:

1. **Homepage (Authority Hub)**
   - Explains who you serve and what market you dominate (e.g., "Ventura County Homes" or "Downtown Chicago Lofts").
   - Features clear CTAs ("Get Market Updates," "Book a Consultation").
   - Links to lead magnets like free reports or calculators.
2. **Pillar Pages (Search-Intent Focused)**
   - Separate pages for Buyers, Sellers, Investors, and Landlords.
   - Each pillar optimized for high-volume keywords (e.g., "Homes for Sale in Ventura," "How to Sell a Home Fast in Chicago").
   - Include video, FAQs, and internal links to local-area posts.

3. **Local Posts (Hyper-Specific Long-Tail Content)**
   - Blog posts about neighborhoods, market updates, or lifestyle topics ("Top 5 Hidden Gems in Ventura County").
   - Each links back to a relevant pillar page to strengthen topical authority.

Recommended Tools

- **Website Platform:** WordPress + Elementor / Luxury Presence / KvCORE
- **SEO Tools:** SurferSEO | Ahrefs | Google Search Console
- **Analytics:** Google Analytics 4 + Hotjar heatmaps
- **Conversion Plug-ins:** Hello Bar | ConvertBox | Gravity Forms

Plain-English Commentary

Your SEO site is your digital land.

Every page that ranks is a plot producing organic traffic. The more "plots" you develop, content, backlinks, and structure, the more lead income you have.

Section 2: "Rent-to-Own" Digital Funnels

Funnel Framework

These funnels "capture, qualify, and convert" buyers or sellers, then either feed your business or generate revenue by renting the funnel to others.

Stage 1 – Traffic Entry
Ads, social media, or SEO blogs drive users to a landing page offering value ("Free Home Valuation," "See Off-Market Listings").

Stage 2 – Lead Capture
Use simple forms with progressive fields (Name, Email, Phone, Timeline). Incentivize with instant tools (valuation widgets, PDF reports).

Stage 3 – Nurture Sequence
Automated email/SMS follow-up provides value and builds trust. Example:

- Day 1: "Your home valuation results."
- Day 3: "3 Ways to Raise Your Home's Value."
- Day 7: "Ready to discuss selling?"

Stage 4 – Handoff or Monetization

- **Internal use:** route qualified leads to your CRM.
- **External monetization:** license the funnel or sell exclusive leads to partner agents/investors for a fixed fee or monthly retainer.

Recommended Tools

- **Funnel Builders:** GoHighLevel | ClickFunnels | LeadPages
- **Automation:** Zapier | ActiveCampaign | HubSpot Workflows
- **Calendaring:** Calendly | TidyCal | OnceHub
- **Follow-Up Systems:** Twilio | HighLevel SMS | Mailchimp

Plain-English Commentary

Think of funnels as "digital duplexes": you build them once, and they keep producing rent. The more targeted your entry traffic, the higher your ROI per visitor.

Section 3: Licensing and Affiliate Frameworks

Monetization Models

1. **Exclusive Lead Licensing**
    - You sell qualified leads to a single investor or agent within a territory.
    - Example: 50 buyer leads / month × $25 each = $1,250 recurring.
2. **Affiliate Revenue**
    - Partner with lenders, title companies, or relocation services.
    - You earn referral commissions for every client who converts.
3. **Branded Network Portals**
    - Create a niche directory (e.g., "California Coastal Homes") where professionals pay a subscription for featured placement.

Recommended Tools

- **CRM & Lead Routing:** FollowUp Boss | HubSpot | GoHighLevel
- **Affiliate Tracking:** Tapfiliate | FirstPromoter | PartnerStack
- **Payment Processing:** Stripe | PayPal | Chargebee

Section 4: Integration & Automation Stack

Layer	**Purpose**	**Example Tools**
Data Capture	Forms & chat widgets	Typeform · HubSpot Forms · ManyChat
CRM	Lead storage & pipeline tracking	Pipedrive · GoHighLevel · FollowUp Boss
Automation	Sequences & triggers	Zapier · ActiveCampaign · Make
Analytics	Performance tracking	Google Analytics · Looker Studio
Monetization	Billing & partner payouts	Stripe · Chargebee

Plain-English Commentary

Digital funnels and licensing models are the "software" version of the control model. Instead of managing roofs and tenants, you manage traffic and data, and the rent you collect is a lead.

Section 5: AI-Powered Funnel Optimization & Predictive Analytics

How Artificial Intelligence Is Rewriting Digital Deal Flow

The next generation of invisible investors will not just build funnels, they'll train them.

AI has transformed how digital assets see, score, and scale opportunities. Instead of waiting for conversions, smart systems can now predict intent, personalize offers, and allocate ad spend dynamically.

1. Predictive Lead Scoring

AI tools now analyze hundreds of behavioral signals, click depth, dwell time, form hesitation, and response patterns, to score each lead's probability to convert.

- **Example:** HubSpot AI and ActiveCampaign's "Predictive Sending" rank and time outreach automatically.
- **Investor advantage:** You focus on the 20% of leads most likely to transact, multiplying ROI on ad spend.

Plain-English Commentary

Instead of manually filtering who's serious, AI does it for you, saving time and eliminating emotional bias from your pipeline.

2. Dynamic Content Personalization

Machine learning can rewrite funnels on the fly. Landing pages and emails can now adjust headlines, CTAs, or offers based on visitor demographics, location, or behavior history.

- **Example Tools:** Mutiny | RightMessage | Systeme.io AI | Jasper Campaigns
- **Real-World Use:** A first-time visitor sees "Discover Your Dream Home," while a repeat visitor sees "Ready to Sell for Maximum Value?"

Plain-English Commentary
Every visitor experiences a custom funnel, turning generic marketing into a one-to-one conversation, at scale.

3. Predictive Media Buying

Platforms like Google Performance Max and Meta Advantage+ now use reinforcement learning to optimize ad placements in real-time.
They evaluate which audiences and creatives perform best, rebalancing budgets hourly.

- **Key Tools:** Google Ads P-Max | Meta Advantage+ | AdCreative.ai | Revealbot
- **Benefit:** No more guessing which ad will perform — algorithms handle allocation and scaling.

Plain-English Commentary

AI is now the "property manager" of your ad dollars, optimizing exposure 24/7 while you sleep.

4. Autonomous Follow-Up & Nurture

AI chatbots and voice systems can now sustain personalized conversations across text, email, and voice without human intervention.

- **Tools:** HighLevel AI | Drift | Tidio | Voiceflow AI | Twilio Autopilot
- **Use Case:** Prospects get follow-ups that feel real — appointment confirmations, market updates, even empathy-based responses.

Plain-English Commentary

Think of this as your "digital inside sales team", tireless, scalable, and trained on your brand voice.

5. Predictive Market Analytics

Data models can now project neighborhood-level price movements, rental yields, or occupancy trends based on real-time feeds.

- **Examples:** PropStream AI | Reonomy Insights | Zillow Zestimate API | Mashvisor Analytics
- **Benefit:** Investors can target properties or partnerships in markets before they trend upward.

Plain-English Commentary
Invisible investors win not by reacting, but by anticipating.

Putting It All Together: The AI Funnel Stack

Stage	AI Function	Example Tools	Result
Attract	Predictive ad buying	Google P-Max · Meta Adv+	Smarter traffic
Capture	Dynamic content personalization	Mutiny · Jasper AI	Higher conversion
Nurture	AI chat + email automation	HighLevel AI · Drift	Continuous engagement
Close	Predictive lead scoring	HubSpot AI · ActiveCampaign	Prioritized deals
Analyze	Market forecasting	PropStream AI · Mashvisor	Strategic insight

The Future Edge

The invisible investor's next competitive edge won't be found in property; it'll be found in pattern recognition.

Owning the data pipeline means owning tomorrow's opportunities. The investor who trains their funnel today will own their market tomorrow.

Appendix C — Recommended Tools & Tech Stack

Your invisible-investing ecosystem: technology, automation, and systems that compound control.

Section 1: Core Business Infrastructure

Category	Purpose	Recommended Tools	Notes
CRM (Customer Relationship Management)	Organize leads, track deals, automate communication.	GoHighLevel · HubSpot · FollowUp Boss	Choose one platform and master it. A CRM is your "digital headquarters."
Email & Automation	Nurture sequences, drip campaigns, and follow-ups.	ActiveCampaign · ConvertKit · Klaviyo	Automate the first 10 days of your lead follow-up — then personalize.
Scheduling & Meetings	Booking calls and consultations.	Calendly · OnceHub · TidyCal	Sync with your CRM to eliminate manual scheduling.
Contract & E-Signature	Drafting and executing partnership agreements.	PandaDoc · DocuSign · HelloSign	Store signed agreements in a shared cloud folder for compliance.
File Storage & Collaboration	Secure, searchable document management.	Google Drive · Notion · Dropbox	Build organized folders by client, deal, and project.

Section 2: Marketing & Lead Generation Tools

Category	**Purpose**	**Recommended Tools**	**Notes**
Website Builders	Design SEO-ready websites and landing pages.	WordPress + Elementor · Luxury Presence · Squarespace · Webflow	Prioritize speed, mobile optimization, and lead capture forms.
SEO & Analytics	Rank content and monitor performance.	Ahrefs · SurferSEO · Google Analytics 4 · Hotjar	Track keyword growth and conversion behavior monthly.
Funnel Builders	Create and deploy automated sales funnels.	GoHighLevel · ClickFunnels · LeadPages	Templates are leverage, duplicate what works.
Advertising Platforms	Acquire traffic at scale.	Meta Ads Manager · Google Ads · TikTok Ads	Use small budgets to test creative before scaling.
Social Scheduling & Engagement	Manage and automate social content.	Metricool · Buffer · Later · Hootsuite	Automate posting, but keep engagement manual for authenticity.

Section 3: Digital Asset Creation & Monetization

Category	Purpose	Recommended Tools	Notes
Graphic & Video Design	Create visuals, infographics, and social assets.	Canva Pro · Adobe Express · CapCut · Descript	Batch-create branded assets once a month.
Affiliate & Partner Tracking	Manage commissions and referral payouts.	PartnerStack · Tapfiliate · FirstPromoter	Use unique tracking links to automate revenue splits.
Payment Gateways	Process transactions and subscriptions.	Stripe · Chargebee · PayPal Business	Automate recurring payments for licensing or leads.
Membership & Learning Platforms	Build courses or paid networks.	Kajabi · Circle · Skool	Recurring memberships = digital rent.
Marketplace Builders	Create local vendor or referral directories.	Sharetribe · Tiledesk · Softr	Build niche platforms (e.g., "California Coastal Agents").

Section 4: AI & Automation Stack

Category	**Purpose**	**Recommended Tools**	**Notes**
Content Creation AI	Write SEO blogs, listings, and ad copy.	Jasper · Writesonic · ChatGPT	Train your AI on tone and local market language.
Automation & Integration	Connect apps and workflows.	Zapier · Make (Integromat) · Pabbly	Build "if this, then that" automations, set them once, and refine monthly.
Predictive Analytics & Forecasting	Anticipate market shifts and optimize funnels.	Reonomy AI · Mashvisor · PropStream	Use data to stay six months ahead of market trends.
Ad Optimization & Creative AI	Auto-test creatives and optimize ads.	AdCreative.ai · Revealbot · Pencil AI	These tools reduce your creative cost per lead dramatically.
AI CRM Enhancements	Lead scoring, timing, and smart follow-up.	HubSpot AI · Salesforce Einstein · GoHighLevel AI	Let algorithms tell you who to call, and when.

Section 5: Operational Systems & Outsourcing

Category	**Purpose**	**Recommended Tools**	**Notes**
Virtual Assistants & Freelancers	Delegate admin, marketing, and data work.	Upwork · OnlineJobs.ph · Fiverr Business	Start small with repetitive tasks, SOP everything.
Process Documentation	Create repeatable systems and checklists.	Notion · Trainual · Process Street	Document every workflow once; refine over time.
Team Communication	Centralize collaboration and updates.	Slack · Microsoft Teams · Basecamp	Keep external partners in shared channels.
Project Management	Track deliverables and deadlines.	ClickUp · Asana · Trello · Monday.com	Create recurring templates for new projects or deals.
Accounting & Financial Management	Manage income, expenses, and taxes.	QuickBooks Online · Xero · Wave	Reconcile monthly — automate reporting when possible.

Section 6: Bonus — The Invisible Investor Stack Framework

The 5-Layer System Map:

1. **Capture Layer** — Funnels, forms, and lead magnets
2. **Convert Layer** — CRM, automations, and sequences
3. **Control Layer** — Partnership contracts and management systems
4. **Cashflow Layer** — Payment, licensing, and affiliate systems
5. **Compass Layer** — Analytics, forecasting, and market intelligence

Plain-English Insight

Each layer builds upon the next. The more you systemize, the less you supervise. Your tech stack becomes your digital workforce, compounding 24/7 without payroll.

Appendix D — Worksheets and Frameworks

Each worksheet in this section is designed to help you turn theory into practice, to move from insight to implementation, from control to cash flow. These frameworks can be completed digitally or printed and used as physical worksheets for strategic reflection.

Section 1: Find Your Leverage Type

Purpose: Identify your dominant Invisible Investor archetype, Connector, Controller, Creator, or Collaborator.
Instructions: For each statement below, rate yourself from 1 (rarely true) to 5 (always true).

Circle statements that feel natural; they'll reveal your core leverage type.

Statement	**Rating (1–5)**
I'm skilled at connecting people who can benefit from knowing each other.	
I find fulfillment in managing and optimizing systems or assets.	
I enjoy building online tools, content, or platforms that attract people.	
I'm good at creating win-win deals and collaborations.	
I prefer flexibility and low risk over heavy financial investment.	
I often see value that others overlook in relationships or information.	

Statement	Rating (1–5)
I can visualize processes and build structure from chaos.	
I naturally attract others to work with or learn from me.	

Scoring Guide:

- Mostly 1s & 2s in connection-related statements → **Connector**
- Mostly 1s & 2s in operations/system statements → **Controller**
- Mostly 1s & 2s in content/creation statements → **Creator**
- Mostly 1s & 2s in collaboration/equity statements → **Collaborator**

Insight: Your leverage type determines where to start, but not where you'll stay. Most Invisible Investors eventually blend at least two archetypes.

Section 2: Map Your Ecosystem

Purpose: Visualize your network, partnerships, and influence flow.

Instructions:
Draw a circle in the center labeled **"You."**
Surround it with three outer layers:

1. **Inner Circle:** trusted collaborators, mentors, or key partners.
2. **Middle Circle:** recurring relationships (clients, vendors, affiliates).

3. **Outer Circle:** extended reach (followers, subscribers, brand audience).

Reflection Questions:

- Where does most of your opportunity flow from today?
- Who are the five people that have created the most leverage in your life or business?
- Which relationships could become profit partnerships with the right structure?

Insight: Your network is your invisible balance sheet. Leverage increases when you add structure, intention, and reciprocity to your relationships.

Section 3: Equity Without Capital

Purpose: Quantify how your skill set can earn equity or profit participation in deals.

Exercise:
List three current or potential partnerships where your expertise could replace capital contribution.

Deal / Partner	Value You Provide	% Equity or Profit Share	Time Commitment	Potential Annual ROI

Reflection Questions:

- Where are you currently being paid once for work that could earn recurring income instead?

- Which skill or service creates the most leverage for others — and how can you monetize it as equity?

Insight: Every skill can be turned into a stake. Stop trading time for transactions; start trading talent for participation.

Section 4: Control-Based Cash Flow Calculator

Purpose: Model potential returns from non-ownership-based strategies.

Model	Initial Investment	Monthly Gross	Monthly Net	% ROI	Notes
Master Lease	$	$	$	%	
Management Contract	$	$	$	%	
Digital Lead System	$	$	$	%	
Affiliate or Partner Split	$	$	$	%	
Equity Collaboration	$	$	$	%	

Instructions:

1. Input your projected numbers for each control model.
2. Calculate ROI = (Net ÷ Investment) × 100%.
3. Identify which models have the highest scalability and lowest time burden.

Insight: ROI isn't just a number, it's a mirror of how efficiently you control value.

30-DAY ACTION PLAN: Becoming the Invisible Investor

Purpose: To give you a measurable, step-by-step roadmap for transforming knowledge into leverage, building income and influence within 30 days.

Week 1 – Rewire Your Mindset

- Audit your beliefs around ownership and security.
- Identify all current income streams tied to ownership vs. control.
- Choose your starting archetype (Connector, Controller, Creator, or Collaborator).
- Create your first Influence Inventory: people, platforms, and skills that can generate leverage.

Outcome: Awareness. You'll see how control, not ownership, drives wealth.

Week 2 – Build Your First Control Asset

- Launch one control-based venture: a referral network, operational contract, or digital funnel.
- Write a one-page agreement defining the exchange of value and responsibilities.
- Set up your foundational tech stack (CRM, scheduling, communication tools).
- Automate one repetitive process in your business or marketing.

Outcome: Implementation. You've created a controllable income-producing mechanism.

Week 3 – Monetize and Multiply

- Introduce a paid component: referral fees, management income, or digital monetization.
- Track KPIs (contacts, conversions, hours saved).
- Identify two complementary archetypes to layer in (e.g., a Connector adding Creator systems).
- Document learnings in your Invisible Portfolio Tracker.

Outcome: Momentum. Your system is now generating measurable income.

Week 4 – Systemize and Scale

- Create a repeatable workflow using automation or virtual assistants.
- Build your first recurring income stream that operates without daily input.
- Map your 6-month expansion plan: new relationships, digital assets, or collaborations.
- Reflect: What control do you hold now that you didn't have 30 days ago?

Outcome: Autonomy. You've moved from operator to architect, from participant to producer.

Completion Outcome

By the end of 30 days, you will have

✅ Built at least one recurring, control-based income stream.

✅ Created your first personal ecosystem map.

✅ Quantified your equity potential through skill leverage.

✅ Begun shifting your identity from owner to orchestrator, from investor to Invisible Investor

Appendix E — Case Studies & Real-World Examples

Proof that control-based investing is already reshaping how wealth is built.

Each example below demonstrates one of the four Invisible Investor archetypes: **Connector, Controller, Creator, and Collaborator**, operating in real markets today. None of these entities relies primarily on property deeds for wealth creation. Their assets are influence, systems, and scale.

Case Study 1 — The Connector: Homeward & the Power of Transaction Control

Model in Action:
Homeward (Austin, TX) acts as a bridge between buyers and sellers by fronting cash offers for clients who haven't yet sold their homes. Instead of owning homes long-term, Homeward earns through transaction fees and short-term capital velocity.

Invisible Investor Mechanics:

- Controls the moment of the deal without holding the asset.
- Monetizes speed, certainty, and reputation instead of square footage.
- Uses lender and agent partnerships for reach rather than inventory.

Lesson:
You don't need deeds to dominate an industry; you need to own timing and trust in the transaction flow.

Case Study 2 — The Controller: Sonder & the Master-Lease Revolution

Model in Action:
Sonder leases multifamily and hotel units long-term, redesigns them for short-term stays, and profits from the rental spread. The company manages thousands of units globally while owning almost none of the underlying properties.

Invisible Investor Mechanics:

- Master-lease agreements = control without capital outlay.
- Revenue from hospitality operations, not appreciation.
- Data analytics determine where to lease and when to exit.

Lesson:
Control gives optionality. Ownership gives an obligation. Sonder scales because it controls experiences, not structures.

Case Study 3 — The Creator: BiggerPockets & the Monetization of Knowledge

Model in Action:
BiggerPockets began as a real estate blog and forum.

It now generates seven-figure revenue through memberships, advertising, courses, and lead referrals, without buying a single property.

Invisible Investor Mechanics:

- Built "digital land" that hosts the conversation about real estate.
- Earns recurring revenue from ads and affiliate deals.

- Sells access to information rather than assets.

Lesson:
Information is the new equity. Create the marketplace, and owners will pay rent to reach your audience.

Case Study 4 — The Collaborator: Property Managers as Equity Partners

Model in Action:
Across the U.S., boutique property-management firms are shifting from fee-for-service to profit-sharing partnerships with owners.

One example, Atlas Real Estate Partners, earns small equity stakes in each building it operates, trading management for ownership slices.

Invisible Investor Mechanics:

- Converts expertise into participation.
- Reduces churn by aligning incentives with owners.
- Builds portfolio value without new capital injections.

Lesson:
Collaboration compounds faster than capital. When service becomes equity, loyalty becomes legacy.

Case Study 5 — Hybrid Models: Airbnb Hosts as Micro-Controllers

Model in Action:
Thousands of Airbnb operators lease apartments via corporate housing agreements and re-rent them. They operate like miniature Sonder-style businesses, leveraging short-term demand against fixed rents.

Invisible Investor Mechanics:

- Arbitrage through operational control.

- Uses dynamic pricing algorithms (e.g., PriceLabs, Wheelhouse).
- Builds a brand portfolio (e.g., "Coastal Lofts Ventura").

Lesson:
The new generation of investors earns through spread management, not speculation.

Case Study 6 — Digital Brokerages & The Equity of Brand

Model in Action:
Platforms like Realty ONE Group and EXP Realty expanded globally by franchising systems, technology, and culture, not brick-and-mortar offices. Agents own their production; the parent companies own the platform.

Invisible Investor Mechanics:

- Digital infrastructure replaces physical expansion.
- Revenue from licensing, transaction fees, and stock programs.
- Culture and technology as scalable equity.

Lesson:
When your system is the product, growth has no geographic limits.

Case Study 7 — Affiliate Marketing Meets Real Estate

Model in Action:
Niche sites like HomeLight and UpNest connect homeowners to vetted agents, earning referral fees per closed deal. They own the funnel, not the agents or listings.

Invisible Investor Mechanics:

- SEO-driven lead generation.

- Monetizes introductions at scale.
- AI matching improves conversion rates.

Lesson:
In the control economy, introductions are inventory. Data is the new deed.

Case Study 8 — The Future Controller: Tokenized Property Platforms

Model in Action:
Companies like RealT and Lofty AI tokenize real-estate ownership, letting investors buy fractional shares of income streams. Operators manage properties; token holders trade liquidity.

Invisible Investor Mechanics:

- Smart contracts execute rent distributions automatically.
- Operators earn fees for curation and management.
- Value stored in blockchain-based access, not physical control.

Lesson:
Tomorrow's controller won't own property; they'll own protocols.

Case Study 9 — AI Consultants as Digital Collaborators

Model in Action:
AI specialists are partnering with developers to optimize pricing, marketing, and occupancy. Rather than billing hourly, they negotiate a profit-share on performance improvement.

Invisible Investor Mechanics:

- Trades data science for equity.

- Measurable impact → measurable stake.
- Creates an infinitely scalable consulting model.

Lesson:
The new "developer" may never pick up a hammer; they build with algorithms.

Case Study 10 — The Invisible Portfolio in Practice

Model in Action:
An independent investor operates three control models simultaneously:

- A digital lead-generation site licensed to agents.
- A master-lease portfolio of five furnished apartments.
- A profit-share partnership with a renovation contractor.

Each system runs semi-autonomously, producing recurring income across different asset types.

Invisible Investor Mechanics:

- Diversified control reduces risk.
- Cross-promotion between assets amplifies visibility.
- Time leveraged through automation and delegation.

Lesson:
The goal isn't to own everything, it's to orchestrate everything.

Summary Insight

Control is the new capital.

These examples prove that in the modern real-estate economy, access, information, and influence outperform ownership, debt, and inventory.
Invisible investors don't collect deeds; they collect systems.

Afterword

There is a quiet revolution happening in the world of real estate and wealth creation. It is not noisy. It does not live on the front page of financial news or the highlight reels of social media.

It is happening in the conversations between innovators, in the spreadsheets of small operators, and in the systems quietly working in the background, the movement of those who have learned that control creates freedom faster than ownership ever could.

You can see it in public dashboards that show proof instead of promises, in simple agreements that align incentives, and in teams that ship value without adding weight.

For decades, we were told that the only path to financial independence was to own more, more property, more inventory, more responsibility.

But ownership has weight. It demands capital, attention, and often, compromise.

Control, on the other hand, multiplies. It adapts. It empowers. Control converts attention into outcomes and outcomes into receipts. It asks better questions,

How can we add value without adding burden?

Distribution that you can redirect beats debt that you must service. The new measure is freedom per unit of responsibility, not square footage per person.

The Invisible Investor does not chase titles or trophies. They architect outcomes. They earn through collaboration, influence, and systems that never sleep. They build portfolios made of partnerships, not properties, ecosystems of leverage instead of liabilities.

Their assets are playbooks, audiences, and agreements that anyone on the team can run. Their reports track renewal, referral, and reach, not just rent and repairs. Their moat is trust that is easy to verify and hard to fake.

This movement is not limited to real estate.

It is reshaping how creators, consultants, entrepreneurs, and professionals think about wealth. The lines between investor, operator, and innovator are blurring, and that is the point. One person can raise demand in the morning, operate fulfillment by noon, and negotiate profit share in the afternoon.

The common thread is repeatable design, not title. This book gives you a working vocabulary for that design and a set of practices you can apply on day one.

The future belongs to those who understand that influence is infrastructure, that data is the new deed, and that freedom lives in control.

Influence that is earned and documented becomes collateral.
Data that is organized and permissioned becomes access equity.

Control that is transparent becomes scale without backlash.

Maybe your first system is small, a single partnership, a lead funnel, or a short-term rental under a master lease. Maybe it starts with a conversation, an idea, or a single spreadsheet. That is how every invisible empire begins, quietly, intelligently, intentionally.

So, take what you have learned here and start where you are. Design systems that align with your skills.

Form partnerships that reward mutual success. Build digital assets that work when you do not. Create equity where others only see effort. Protect your reputation like titles and treat your metrics like truth. Measure progress in velocity, not volume, and in options created, not obligations added.

Because the truth is, the most powerful form of wealth is the one you do not have to be seen to own. And the most successful investors of the next decade will not be the ones with the biggest portfolios. They will be the ones who can create value from anywhere. They will leave a trail that partners can audit and a path that teams can follow. They will prove that freedom is a design decision.

Welcome to The Invisible Movement.

— Jay R. Pocius

Made in the USA
Monee, IL
04 November 2026

67381179R00154